Blackwork Made Easy

Techniques, Patterns & Samplers

Blackwork Made Easy

Techniques, Patterns & Samplers

Lesley Wilkins

SEARCH PRESS

First published in Great Britain 2012

Search Press Limited
Wellwood, North Farm Road,
Tunbridge Wells, Kent TN2 3DR

Reprinted 2013

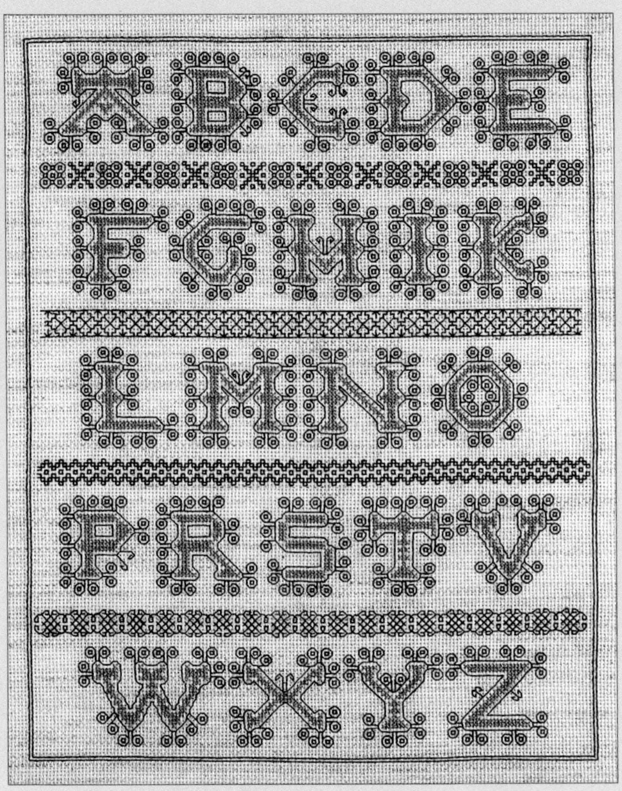

Based on the following books published by Search Press:

Beginner's Guide to Blackwork by Lesley Wilkins, 2002
Traditional Blackwork Samplers by Lesley Wilkins, 2004

Photographs by Charlotte de la Bédoyère and Jon Firth,
Search Press Studios

ISBN: 978-1-84448-753-0

Suppliers
If you have difficulty in obtaining any of the materials and equipment mentioned in this book, then please visit the Search Press website: www.searchpress.com

You are also invited to visit Lesley Wilkins' website:
www.theblackworkguild.com

Publisher's note
All the step-by-step photographs in this book feature the author, Lesley Wilkins, demonstrating blackwork embroidery. No models have been used.

Printed in Malaysia

Contents

Introduction

Blackwork is a counted thread method of embroidery, using straight stitches in a contrasting colour worked on evenweave fabric. The true origin of this type of embroidery appears to have been the Moors and Arabs, who in the 13th century travelled to England with soldiers and noblemen returning from the Crusades.

It is believed that the Spanish princess, Katharine of Aragon, brought blackwork to England with her in 1501. She later married Henry VIII, and for more than twenty years she influenced the English court with her passion for embroidery. The stitch she used was known as 'Spanishwork'. It had become part of Spanish culture through the Moors.

Many blackwork patterns were inspired by Tudor knot gardens and mazes. Knot gardens featured designs of interlacing bands and ribbons made from low hedges, enclosing beds filled with flowers.

There were many portraits painted at this time showing people wearing clothes decorated with blackwork embroidery. One of the blackwork stitches was named after Henry VIII's court painter, Holbein, because so many of his sitters displayed it.

Blackwork's closely textured stitching was not only decorative – it was also used to reinforce collars and cuffs, and to disguise dirt during a time of poor hygiene. The poorer classes also stitched the delicate designs on their clothes as a cheaper alternative to lace.

After Katharine's divorce from Henry in 1533, the Spanish influence disappeared, so the term 'blackwork' replaced 'Spanishwork'.

Before the advent of printed pattern books in 1523 (and in England, not until 1587), band samplers were a means of recording the embroidery patterns used for decorating household linens and clothing. New stitches and patterns were eagerly collected and exchanged between friends by adding them to a sampler. These were worked on narrow strips of plain-weave linen, some of which measured up to 101cm (40in), and recorded embroidered border patterns, most of which were based on repeating motifs.

Patterns which were printed for lacemaking during the Renaissance period showed linear designs that could be adapted for blackwork, and also provided ideas for other types of embroidery. The formal knot garden designs of the Tudor period were another source of inspiration.

A variety of framed band samplers. These were inspired by those made by embroiderers of the past who recorded numerous patterns on cloth before pattern books were available.

When I was ten years old, I discovered blackwork samplers on a visit to the Victoria and Albert Museum in London. That day led to the passion I still have today for blackwork. One of the oldest surviving blackwork samplers, dated 1598, by Jane Bostocke, is kept there. The many patterns recorded on this sampler have been used throughout the designs in this book. I hope that, as you turn the pages of this book, you too will fall in love with blackwork and be inspired to design your own patterns and samplers.

Materials

Fabric

Blackwork requires fabric that is woven evenly in blocks or with a specific number of threads to the inch. Some of the patterns can be very intricate and therefore require a fabric that has a smaller block count to the inch, or a finer thread.

There is a great variety of different fabric and thread colours available. If you are creating a sampler that you want to look aged when it is completed, use off-whites such as antique white, rustico or oatmeal shades in aida. Unbleached or old white linens also give the work an aged feel. The success of a blackwork design depends on a strong contrast between the fabric and the thread, so whatever your colour, choose the thread carefully so that the pattern stands out clearly. With all the variables available to the blackwork embroiderer: in the thickness of the thread, the pattern density and the weight of the fabric, there is not always a need for much colour to create impact.

Aida (block weave)

This is a cotton or cotton mixture fabric and is very practical for counted needlework. It is available in a variety of colours and block counts, with two threads woven into blocks rather than a single thread. It gives accurate results and is ideal for the beginner. The majority of the designs in this book are worked on this fabric.

Evenweave

A plain, single weave fabric with the number of threads for the warp and weft being exactly the same. As the texture is open, the threads are easy to count.

Hardanger

This has pairs of intersecting threads and is easy to count. It is slightly more practical than evenweave as it keeps its shape more firmly.

Needles

For all counted needlework, you will require a blunt needle. Sharp needles will pierce both the threads on the fabric and the stitches already worked. Also, when the needle passes through the fabric, it should not enlarge or distort the hole – if it does, then it is the wrong size. Finer needles have a larger number and thicker needles a lower number. Sizes 22–26 are usually best.

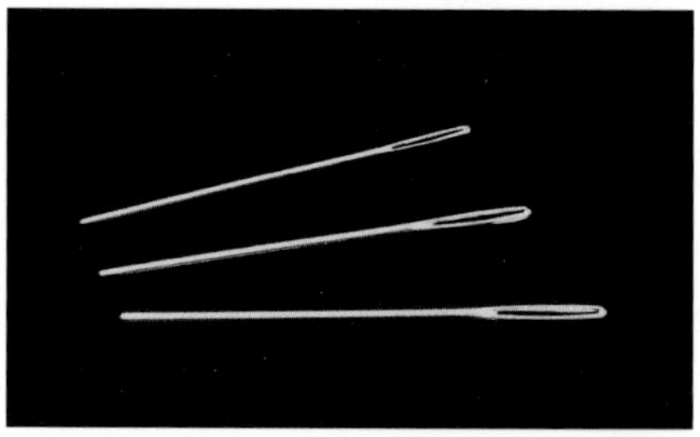

Aida, evenweave and hardanger fabrics. Most of my embroideries are worked on aida, as it is ideal for intricate designs.

Threads

Silk threads were originally used centuries ago, but only by the rich. Now of course, silk threads are available to everyone and there is a greater choice.

Stranded cotton

This is the most popular thread, and the most suitable for blackwork. It has six strands and can be used in many different thicknesses, depending on how many strands are used.

Perle cottons

These come in a variety of thicknesses, from the finest, no. 12 to the thickest, no. 3. An ideal thread for blackwork, with a sheen effect, it is good for outlining.

Coton à broder

This comes in several thicknesses, 40 being the finest and 8 the thickest. It is good for outlining and sits very well on the fabric.

Ordinary machine sewing cotton

This is harder than stranded cotton, and gives fine work a crisp effect.

Cotton perle 5 and 8, coton à broder 16, stranded cotton and ordinary machine cotton, gold lamé and mouline metallised threads with needles in sizes 22, 24 and 26.

Organising your threads

There are many excellent organising systems you can buy, but I make my own cards, which are simple and cost nothing. My method is shown below.

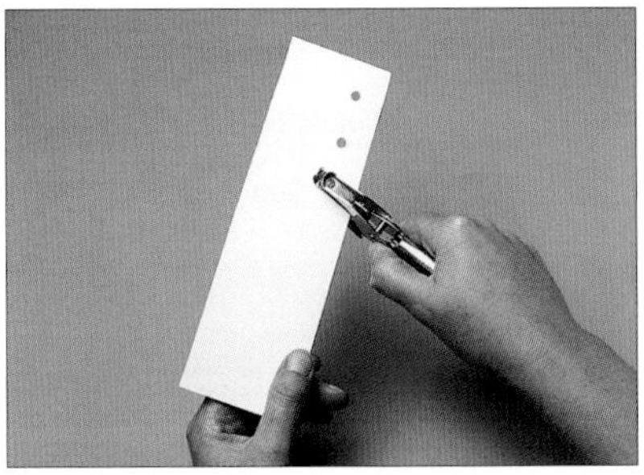

1. Take a piece of stiff card and punch holes down the side.

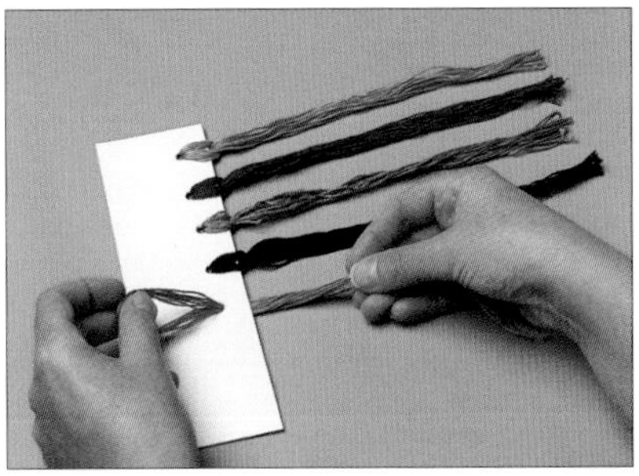

2. Cut your skeins into manageable lengths. Take a length, double it and thread the looped end through a hole in your organiser. Push the cut ends through the loop and pull tight. It is easy to remove one length of thread from the card without disturbing the rest.

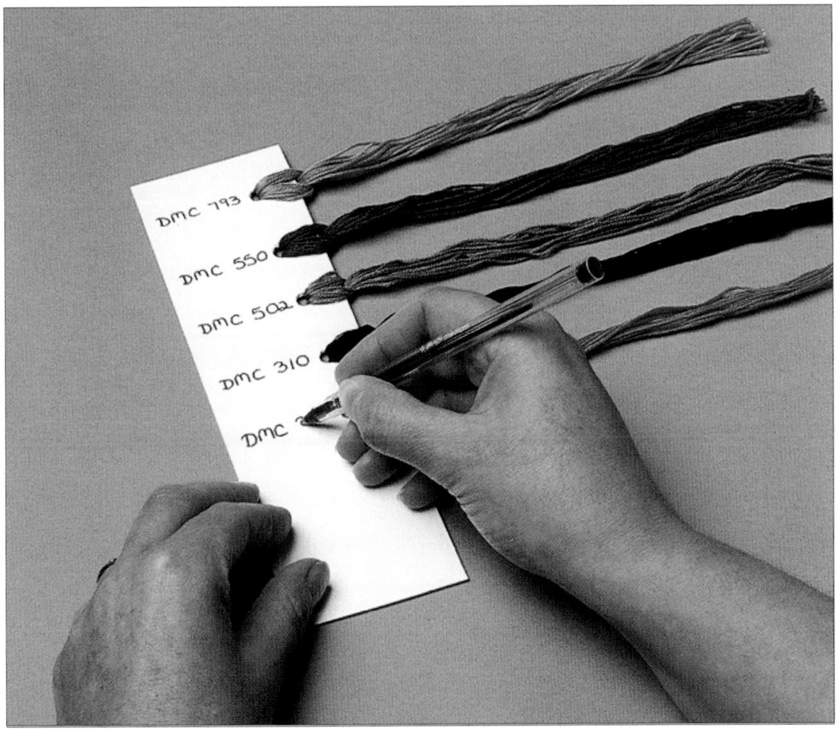

3. At the side of the thread, write the manufacturer's name and the number of the shade. When you have completed your project, any spare thread can be left on the card and used for your next embroidery.

Frames

There are a variety of types to choose from, depending on the size of your fabric. Freestanding frames can now take clip-on magnifiers and lamps, which enable you to have both hands free to sew. Whatever frame you use, the important rule is: always make sure the fabric is drum-tight.

Hoops

These frames are suitable only when the whole of the design fits within the ring area, as stitches can become distorted if you have to move the ring around as you work. The fabric is attached by placing it over the smaller hoop, then forcing the larger hoop over it. The screw should then be tightened to secure the fabric.

Rectangular frame

This frame can accommodate the whole of the fabric width and you can keep the fabric taut throughout by rolling the fabric to the required area and tightening the screws at each corner.

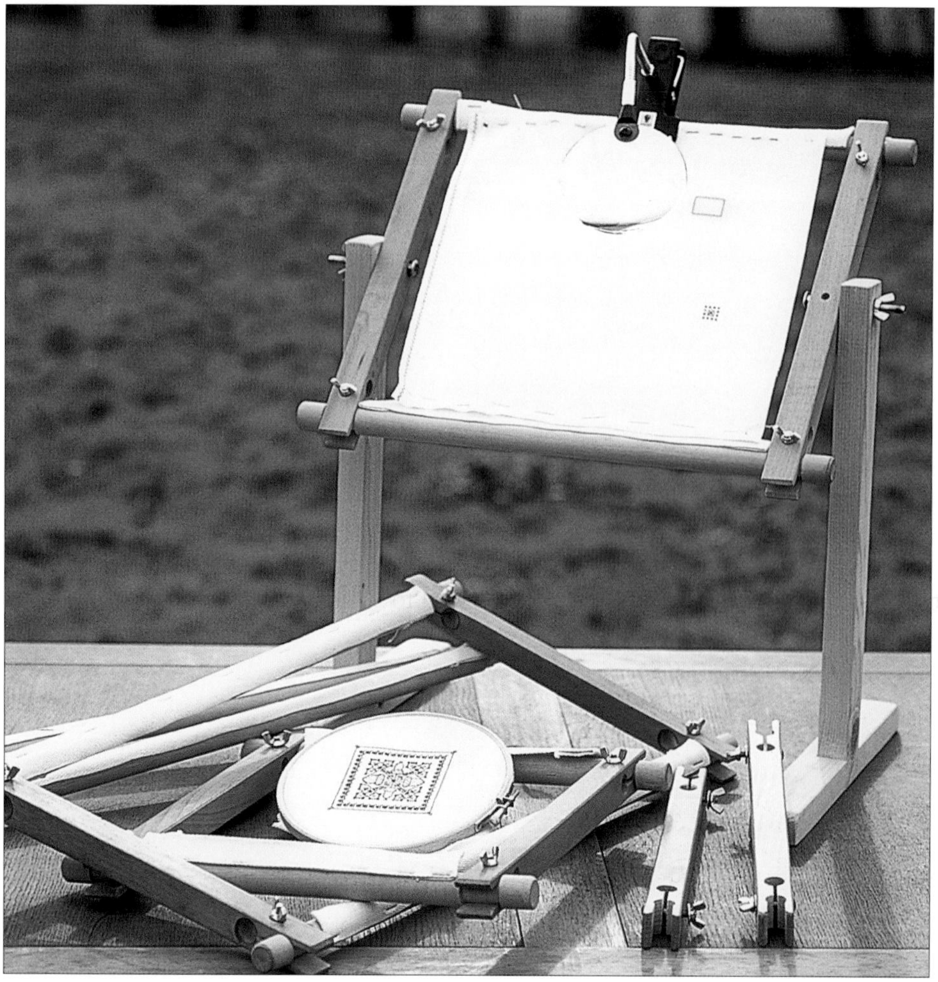

A selection of hand-held rectangular frames and hoops and a seated frame, which allows you to work with both hands free. The clip-on magnifier provides a clearer view for close, intricate patterns. I do not like to work by artificial light, so I always set myself up beside a window.

Other items

A cutting mat, mounting board, picture frame, tape measure, iron, masking tape, ruler, pencil, craft knife, embroidery scissors and dressmaker's scissors.

Embroidery scissors These should be kept sharp to cut the thread in one motion, and the points are useful to unpick mistakes, so they should be fine enough to slip under the stitch and cut it safely.
Dressmaker's scissors To cut the fabric. Always follow the line of the thread to ensure a straight cut.
Tape measure or ruler For choosing fabric size and again when the finished work is to be mounted.
Iron Used to press the finished work before it is mounted.
Pins Used to mark the centre of the fabric before you begin sewing, and to attach the fabric to the edge of the mounting board to keep it in place when lacing or taping the back.
Cutting mat and craft knife These are essential when cutting mounting board.
Acid-free mounting board This is used when mounting your samplers.
Masking tape This prevents the fabric edge from fraying.
Double-sided tape Useful when mounting your finished work.
Picture frame A good frame is the perfect finishing touch for a sampler. The glass can be left in the frame to protect the work from dust, but to prevent the stitches being flattened by the glass, use a card border to rest the glass on or a strip of acid-free mounting board around the inside edge of the frame.

Design

Blackwork is a very creative and flexible form of stitching, made up of straight or diagonal stitches arranged in a huge variety of patterns. This book gives you charts and patterns to work from, but when you become more confident, you may want to create your own designs.

Centuries ago, people were influenced by what they saw in their surroundings. Pattern books were not available until the sixteenth century, which is why the band sampler was created, so that people could keep a record of their designs. Moorish and Arab craftsmen favoured geometric motifs and all-over patterning, which can be found on doorways, mosaic tiles, architecture and other crafts. When these craftsmen became a dominant force in Spain, they influenced the textiles of the country with designs based on grapevines, leaves, roses, pomegranates, heraldic griffins and lions. These motifs, collected over the centuries, were embroidered in black silk on white linen.

If you would like to design your own patterns, carrying a small graph book and pen on your travels is incredibly handy for jotting down ideas. A camera, too, is invaluable to capture instantly on film an idea that can then be worked on when you return home. Ideas for patterns can be found wherever you travel if you look at the buildings that surround you, or even in a simple tile design book. I collect pictures based on a particular subject, such as Tudor knot gardens and mazes which inspired embroiderers of the Renaissance period, and from these I create my own patterns.

Pattern density

Light and dark areas can be created in a design by varying the density of the pattern. Closely worked, dense areas of pattern look darker, but if you eliminate parts of the pattern and open it out, that area will look lighter – see the leaf pattern on the right.

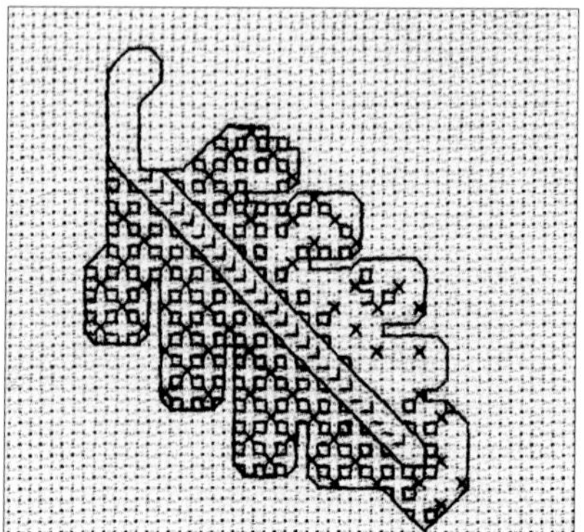

Thread thickness

The more strands of thread you use, the darker and more prominent the design appears, as shown here.

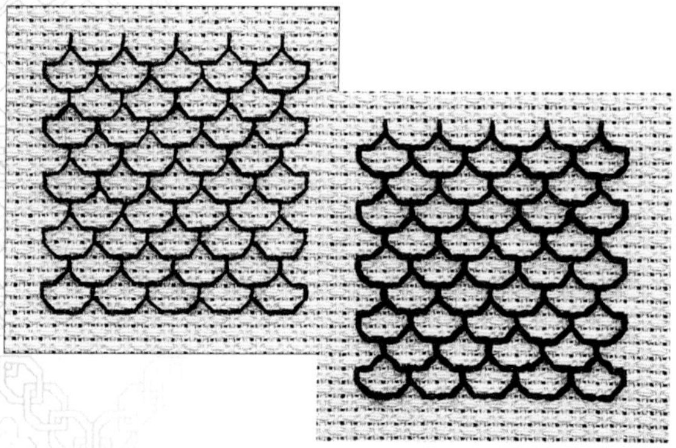

I collected pictures of Tudor knot gardens, which provide design ideas from their intricate, interlocking patterns, and also Moorish tiles, which inspired blackwork of the Renaissance period. Designs inspired by these pictures were then transferred to graph paper.

Working from the sketches above, I created the chart and finally the blackwork sampler shown right. The design at the top echoes the shape of the low-cut hedges which formed knot gardens and mazes. The square Moorish tile design is built up from single motifs on the bottom line, and repeat patterns in the middle.

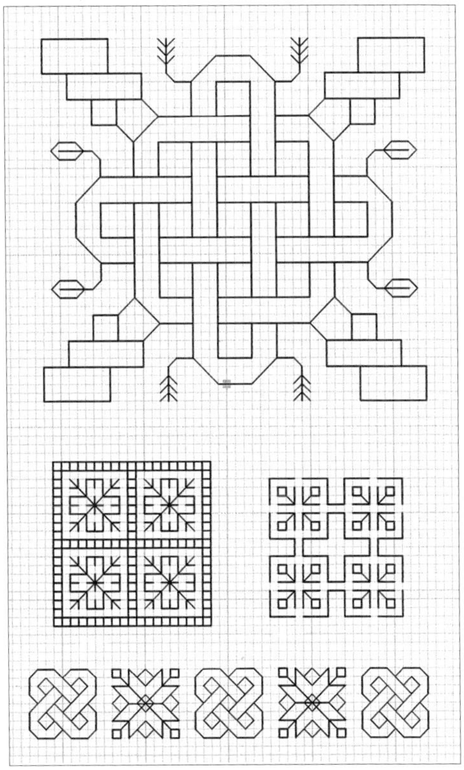

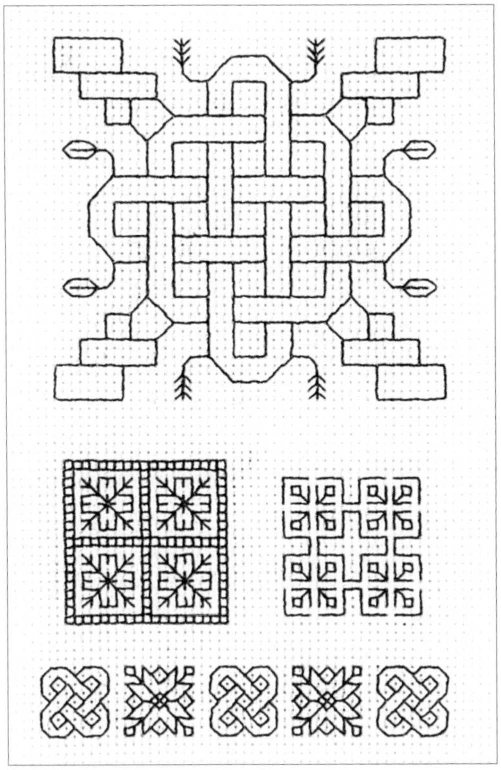

Using charts

The first stitch you place in the fabric when you begin your project can be vital to its success. If you start sewing in the wrong area, you may find halfway through that you have run out of space, and hours of work have been wasted.

On any chart there should be a grey square or black cross to indicate the centre of the design. You can find the centre of your fabric by folding it into four, and this should correspond with the centre mark on the chart.

The chart for the embroidery below is shown opposite. The centre marker can be found below the main flower head. The flower motif is to be sewn first, and this in turn will help you to position the surrounding patterns. One strand of thread has been used throughout the design, but with a variety of colours used to distinguish between the different flower motifs.

A colourful design featuring fuchsias, roses and acorns, inspired by pot displays and pictures in gardening books.

Design size: 8 x 7cm (3 1/8 x 2 3/4in)
Fabric: Aida 16 count, antique white
Threads: DMC Green 904
Pink 3350
Mauve 552
Yellow 742
Brown 801
Use one strand throughout

Getting started

The work station

Every person has their own way of working, holding a frame balanced on their lap or supported by a stand, and sitting on a stool or in a comfortable armchair.

I have a special work box close to hand containing everything I need for that particular project, and I support my frame with a seat frame holder. This enables me to sit comfortably with the frame in my lap, and work freely with both hands.

If you require a magnifier and a lamp attachment, then a floor stand frame would be more beneficial. The most important things to consider are comfort and good back support while you are working, and having your materials close at hand.

Natural daylight is best for embroidery, so sit near a window for the best results. Outdoor sewing can lead to all sorts of disasters, such as dropping the work on the ground or insects getting squashed on the fabric.

If you have to sew at night, work under a good lamp which should be positioned on the left if you are right-handed, or on the right if you are left-handed, to prevent working in your own shadow.

Daylight bulbs, although expensive, are worth investing in and give an excellent clear, natural light.

Seat frames are ideal for embroidery. They enable you to work freely with both hands and you can sit in your comfortable chair in a relaxed position.

A band design typical of the fifteenth and sixteenth centuries. When working on an intricate design like this, I prefer to use a seat frame large enough to hold the whole embroidery at once. This means there is no need to unstretch the fabric and move the embroidery around as work progresses.

Choosing fabric

Having chosen a design, you need to work out how much fabric it will take, by following the guidelines below.

1. Take a ruler or other straight edge to the last stitch on the chart on the left, then the right, and count the squares in between, to find the width. Do the same from top to bottom, to find the height.

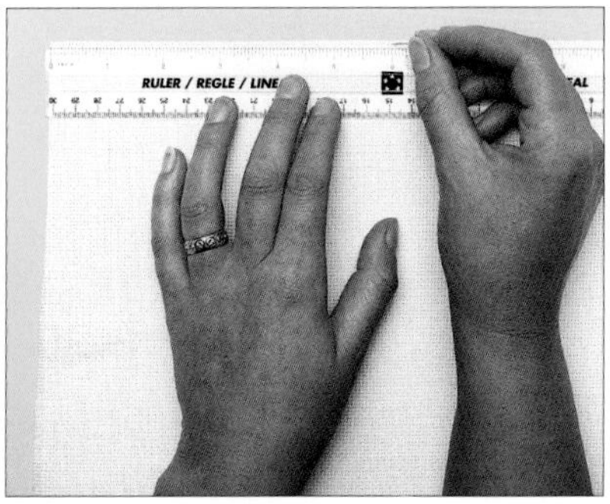

2. To calculate the thread or block count of the fabric, place your ruler on the material and count the number of threads or blocks there are to 2.5cm (1in).

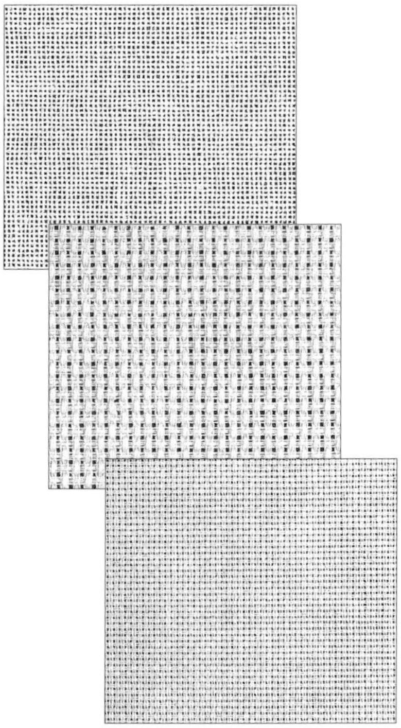

From top to bottom: evenweave, aida and hardanger fabrics.

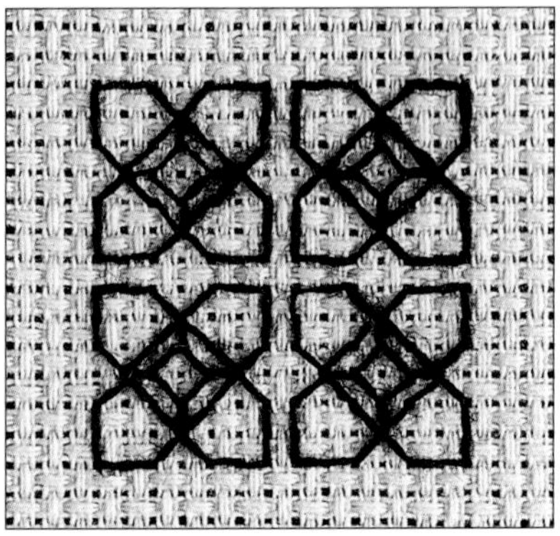

Evenweave is stitched over two threads. So, if there are 26 threads to 2.5cm (1in) and there are two threads to each stitch, that will mean 13 stitches for 2.5cm (1in). If your design has a graph count of 54 squares across and 54 squares down, divide 54 by 13 and you will require 10.5cm^2 ($4\frac{1}{4}$in^2) of fabric.

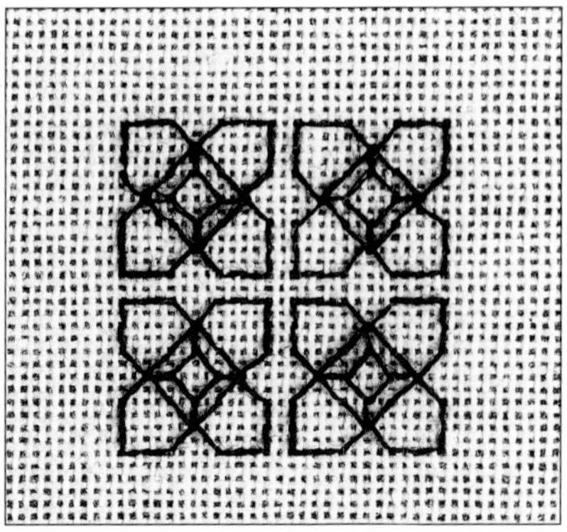

Aida is one stitch per block. So, if your design has a graph count of 54 squares across and 54 squares down, and your aida fabric has 18 blocks to 2.5cm (1in), divide 54 by 18, and you will require a piece of fabric 7.5cm^2 (3in^2).

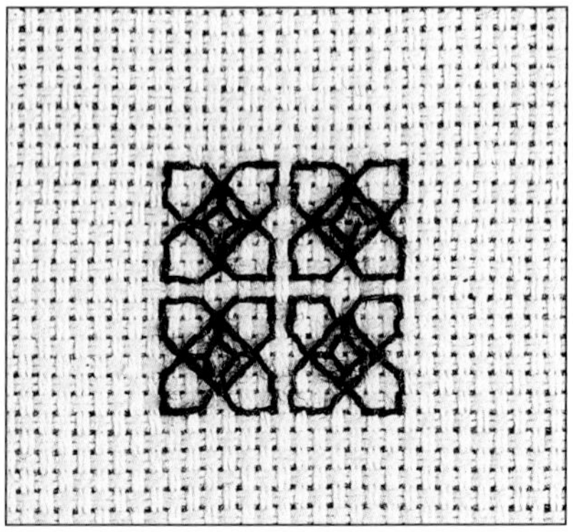

Hardanger is made up of pairs of threads woven together to give a dense background, while still leaving easily visible holes between the warp and weft. It can be stitched over one or two threads. Calculate the size of fabric required in the same way as for aida.

When you are happy with the measurements of the actual sewing area, remember to include extra fabric around your design. I try to leave an extra 10–15cm (4–6in) for stretching and mounting. Smaller projects do not need so much.

It is extremely important to leave extra fabric around the edge of the embroidery, as shown here. This will ensure that you have adequate room to fit the embroidery on the fabric and, when it is finished, to mount and stretch your work around stiff card, ready for display.

Framing

I always work on a rectangular frame because I find it more practical than a hoop. Rolling your design to where you need to sew is easier than constantly removing and replacing a hoop, and the fabric is never distorted, because it is constantly pulled straight and drum tight.

If the fabric you are using frays easily, either hem the edges or tape them with masking tape before sewing the fabric to the webbing.

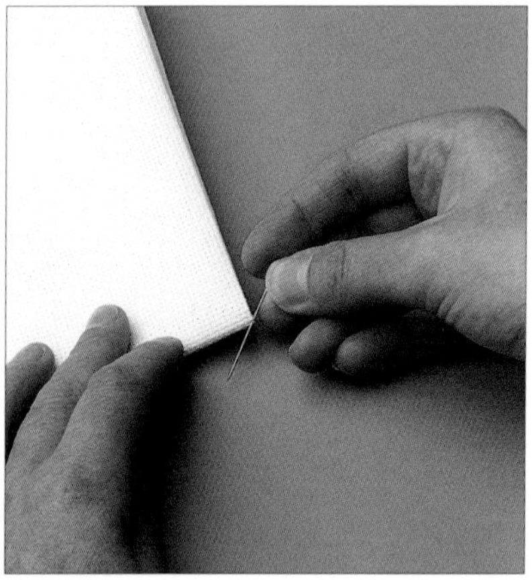

1. Find the centre of the fabric by folding it in half, then in half again. Mark the centre with a pin or a cross stitch.

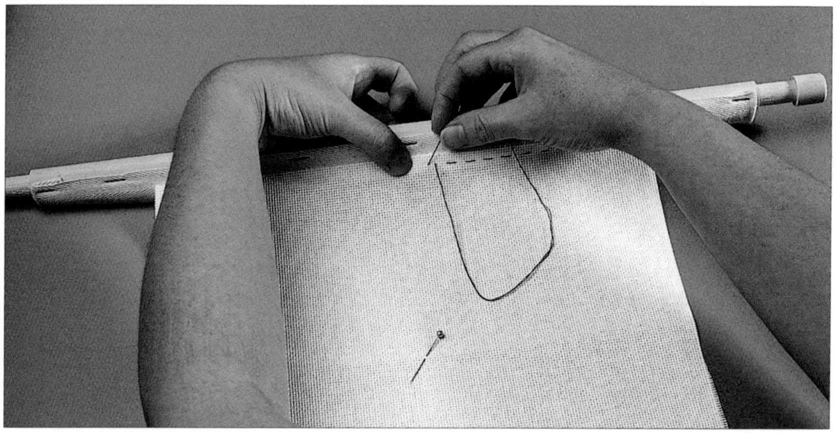

2. Sew the fabric to the top and bottom webbing on the frame with running stitches. Keep the central pin or cross stitch in the centre of the frame, and make sure the fabric does not overlap the width of the frame.

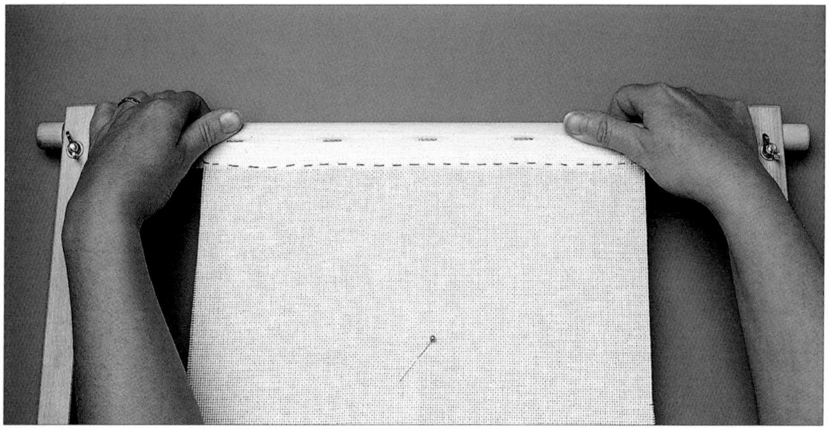

3. Put the frame together and roll the fabric as tightly as possible around the rollers, top and bottom. Keep the fabric centred, and stretch it so that it is drum tight.

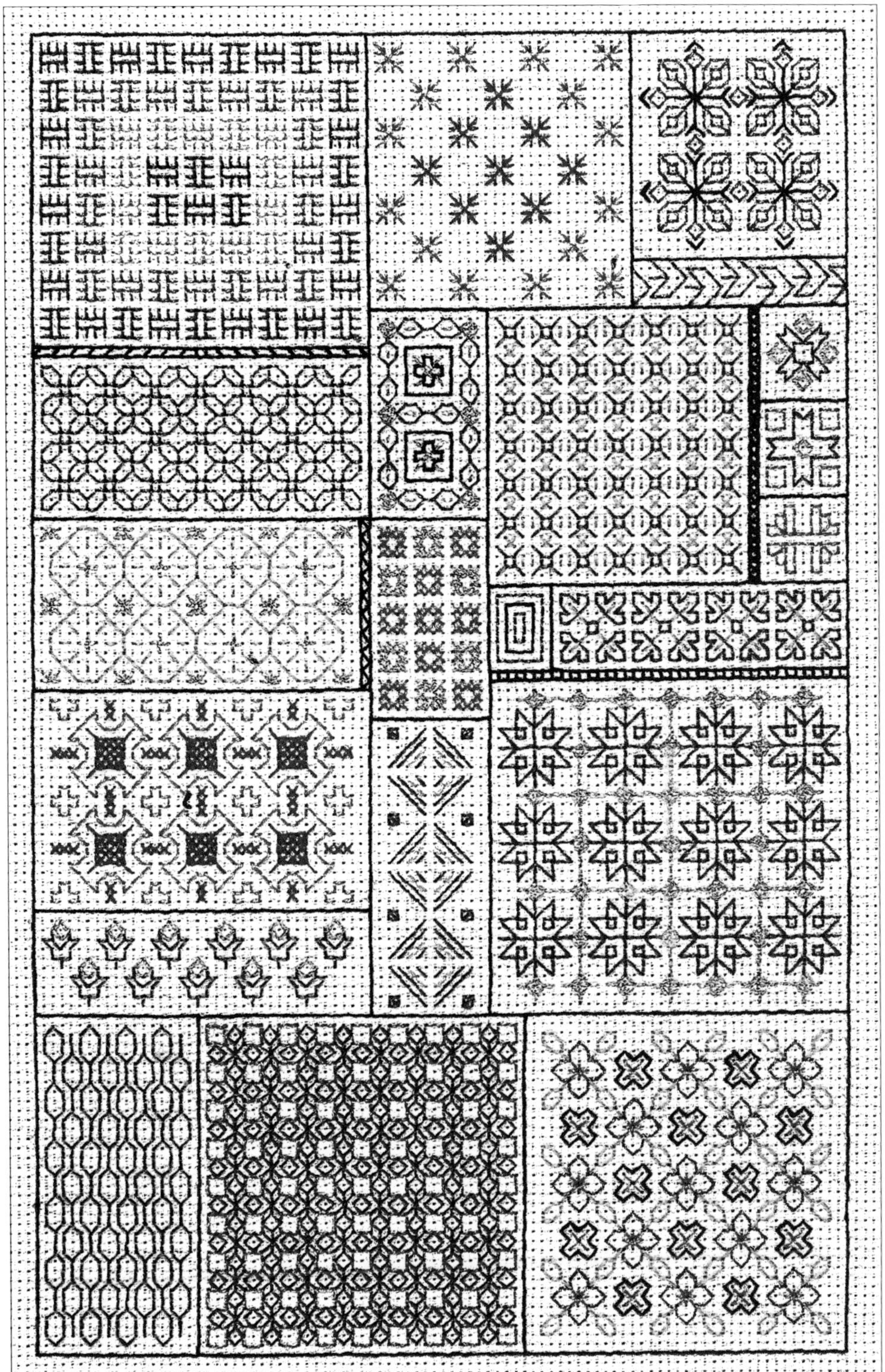

If your design is complicated, like this one, a rectangular frame makes it easier to follow your progress, while keeping the fabric stretched. A hoop frame requires constant adjustment and may distort the fabric and silks.

Stitches

The most common stitches used in blackwork are double running stitch, back stitch and cross stitch. All the projects in this book can be worked using these three stitches.

Double running stitch

Also known as Holbein stitch, this provides a smoother appearance than back stitch and is ideal for intricate geometric patterns.

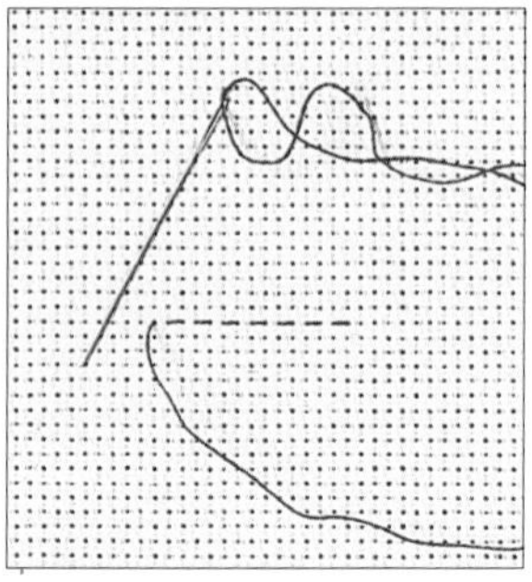

1. Sew a line of running stitches.

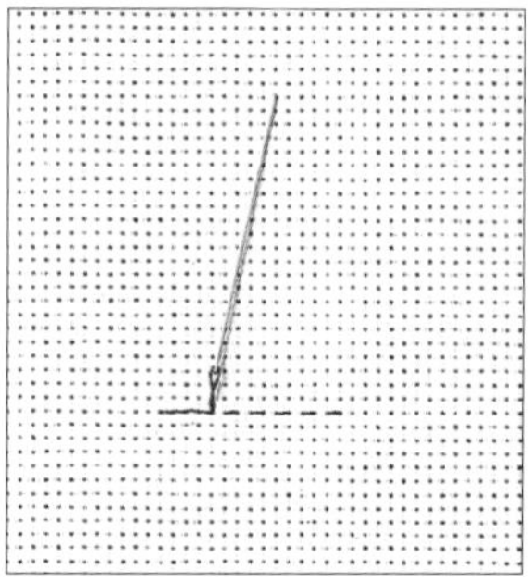

2. Go back along the same line filling in the spaces between the stitches.

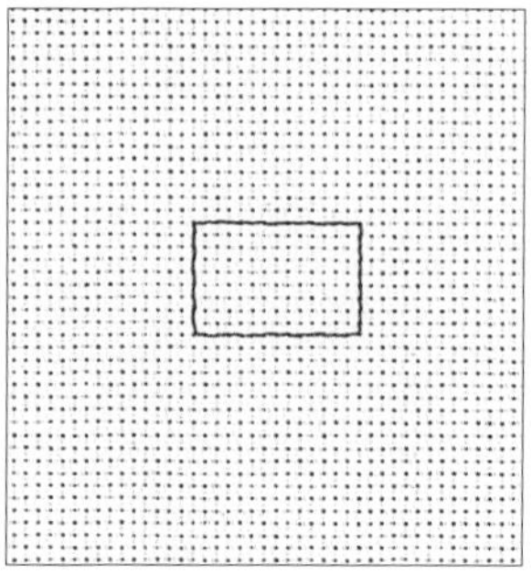

A finished example of double running stitch.

Back stitch

This is used for outlining other stitches as well as in its own right. It gives definition to the design, especially when you are using thicker thread or more than one strand.

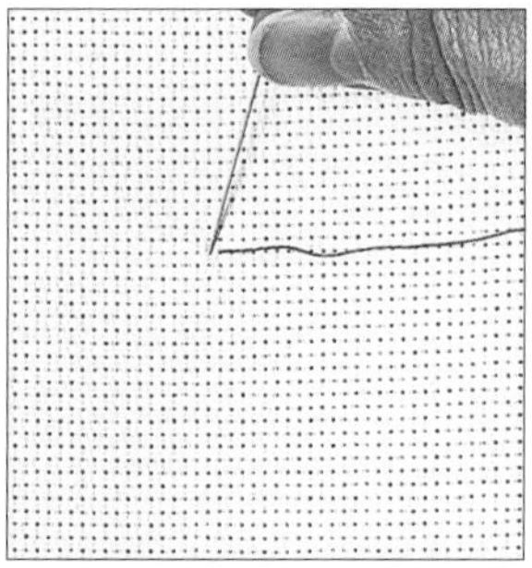

1. Bring the needle up to the right side of the fabric, then take it down to the wrong side at the next point.

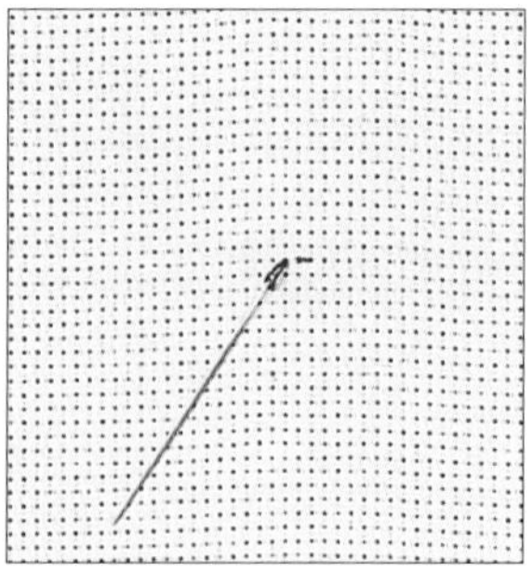

2. At the front of the first stitch, bring the needle up to the right side of the fabric again.

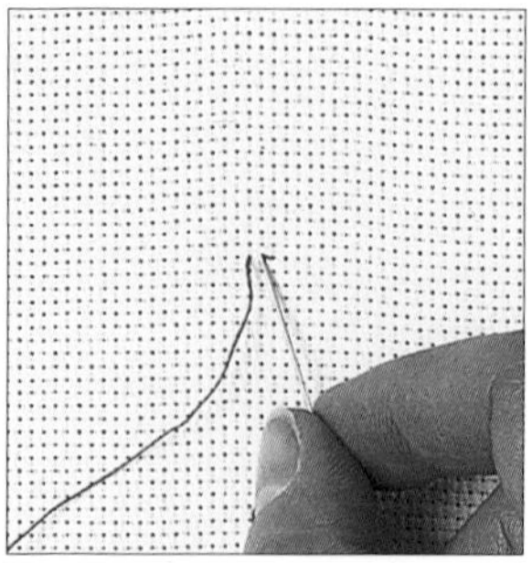

3. Finish the stitch by inserting the needle at the point where the last stitch began.

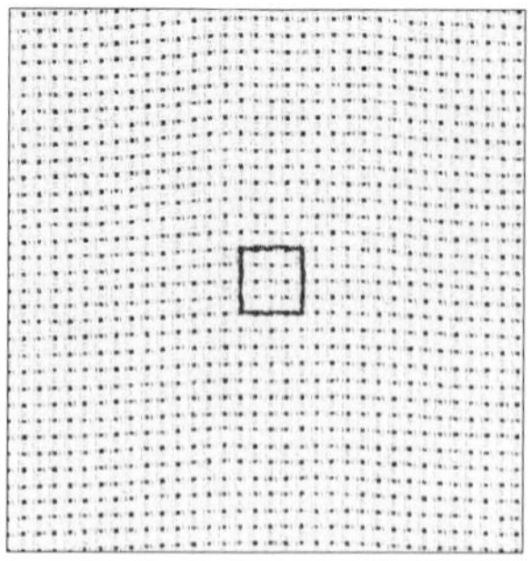

A finished example of back stitch.

Cross stitch

This is the most commonly used counted stitch and is ideal for a variety of patterns and designs. To ensure its neatness, always make sure the top stitch in each cross faces in the same direction.

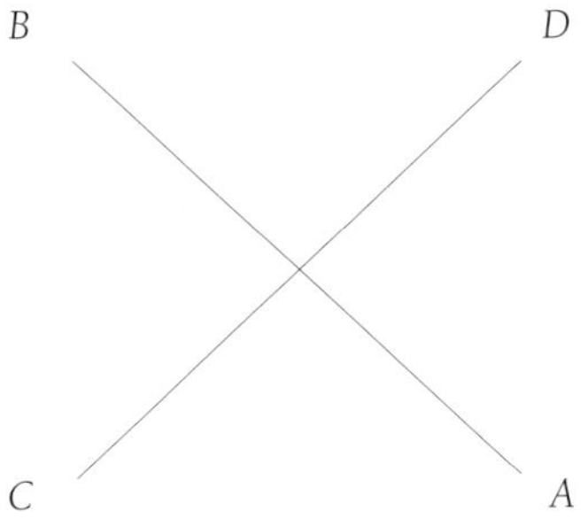

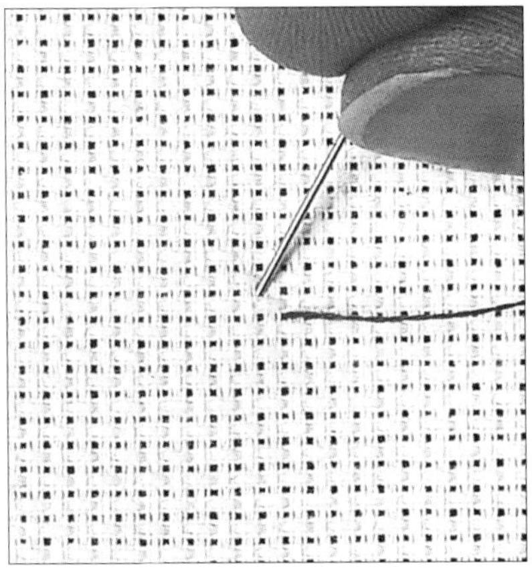

1. Begin at point A. Bring the needle up to the right side of the fabric and insert the needle diagonally at point B.

2. Bring the needle up to the right side of the fabric at point C and insert it down diagonally at point D. For the next stitch, bring the needle up at point C and repeat the procedure.

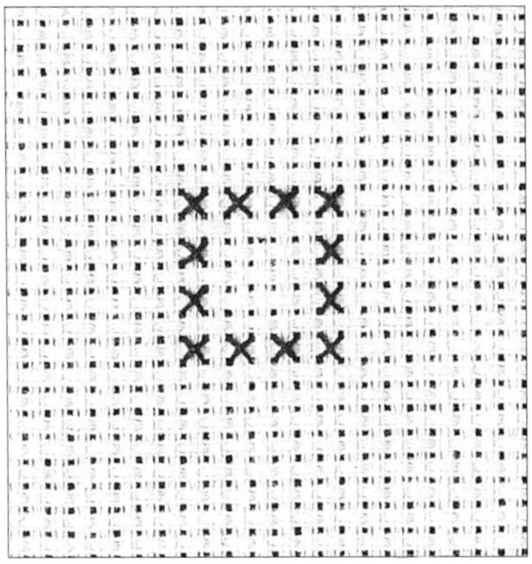

A finished example of cross stitch.

In this framed embroidery, the strawberries were worked in cross stitch, using gold metallic thread. The outline was back stitch and all other parts of the design were worked in double running stitch.

Starting your design

It is important to start at the centre of the chart to ensure that your finished work will be central, with sufficient surplus fabric all around it. The marker on the chart, and the pin or cross stitch you have put in your fabric indicate your starting point.

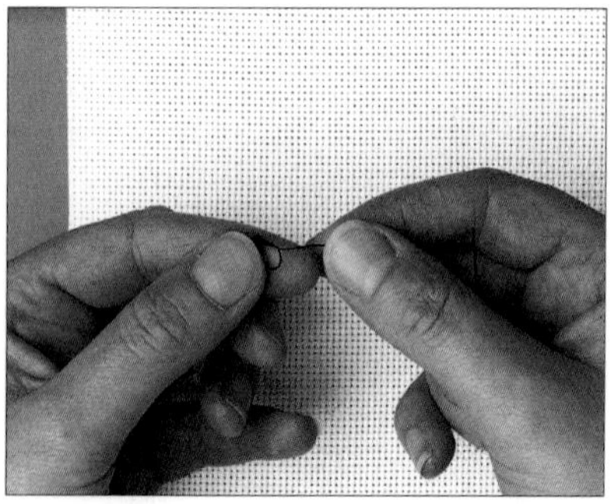

1. Make a knot in your thread. This is a waste knot, and is not permanent, as if not removed later, it would leave an unsightly bump in the surface of your work.

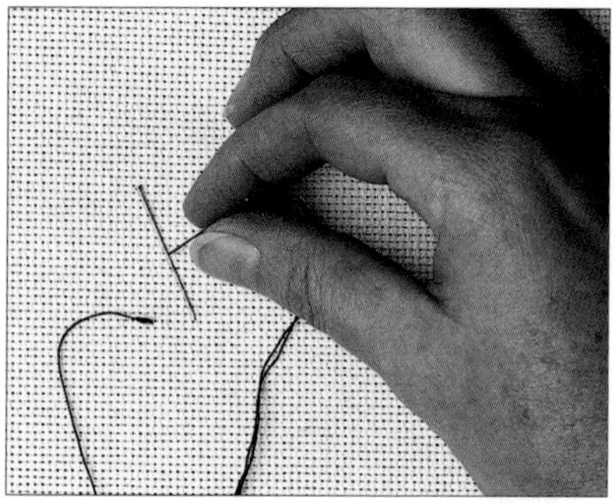

2. Insert the needle from the right side of your work, into an area which will be disguised by a blackwork pattern, not far from the starting point (marked here with a pin).

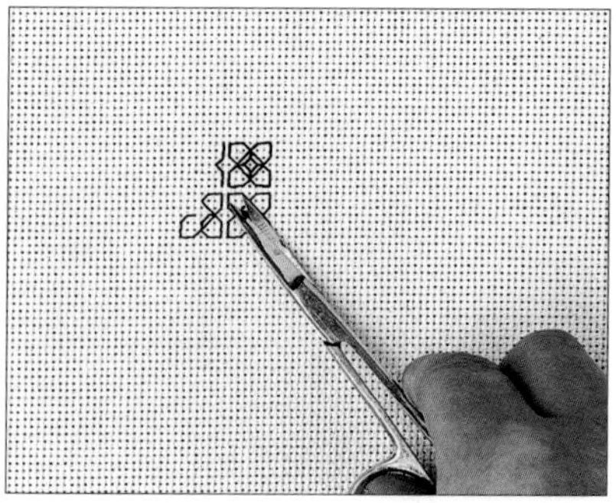

3. Work the area of pattern until you reach the waste knot, cut it off, and continue with the pattern. The thread, which lies at the back of the work, is now secured by the stitches of the pattern. Use this procedure each time you start with a new thread.

Finishing off

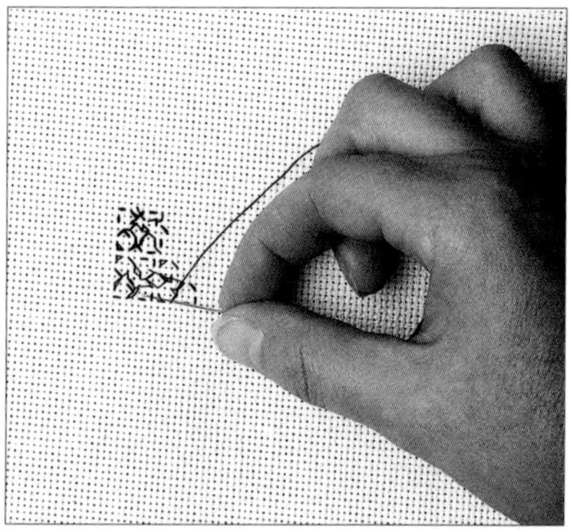

1. Finish a thread by catching two or three stitches underneath, making sure you do not surface on the right side of your work.

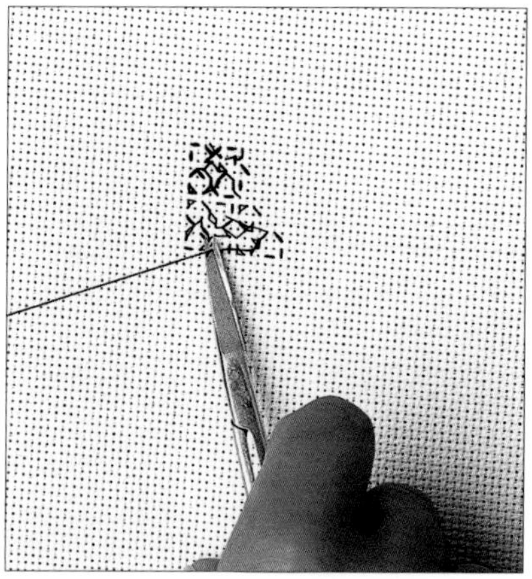

2. Trim off any ends with sharp embroidery scissors.

Hundreds of threads may be started and finished in a design such as this. The important part of any finished embroidery is to ensure that no knots are used. This will allow your work to sit flat without any bumps when mounted. Also, any loose threads left at the back may show through to the right side of the fabric if you have not woven them in correctly.

Flowers and plants

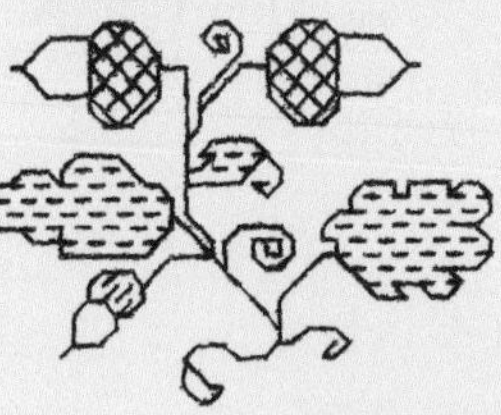

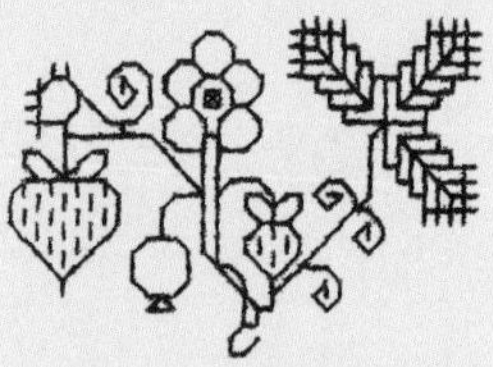

The invention of printing in the mid-fifteenth century provided a ready source of design material for the eager seamstress to sew on to fabric. Illustrations of the plants used by herbalists in their recipes, and of those found growing in Tudor knot gardens and herb gardens, such as roses, pansies, honeysuckle and comfrey, all found their way in to blackwork designs decorating clothes and household furnishings.

A wide range of flower and plant motifs featured in traditional blackwork, with Tudor roses the favourite. These emblems of the Tudor kings were sewn full-face rather than in bud. Carnations, pansies, thistles, tulips, pineapples, figs, grapes and strawberries were also popular. On these and the following pages, the embroidery is shown on the left-hand page, with the chart opposite. Some charts go over several pages. Page 16 explains how to use the charts.

This embroidery shows, on the top row: acorns and a strawberry plant; on the second row: honeysuckle; on the third row: acorns and honeysuckle; on the fourth row: roses and on the bottom row: grapes and a pansy.

This band sampler contains ten examples of patterns that appear on the Jane Bostocke sampler from 1598 – one of the oldest surviving examples (see page 7). It is worked in black and gold threads.

Design size: 31 x 61.7cm (12¼ x 24¼in)

Fabric: Aida 18 count, antique white

Threads: DMC Black 310 (6)
DMC Gold 5282 (1)

Use one strand of black and two strands of gold thread

Chart for the top of the embroidery – this way up

Chart for the middle of the embroidery – this way up

Chart for the bottom of the embroidery – this way up

This sampler was inspired by the pattern layouts of Elizabethan gardens with their mazes and knot gardens, surrounded by roses and grapevines.

Design size: 15 x 40cm (5⁷⁄₈ x 15¾in)
Fabric: Aida 16 count, antique white
Thread: DMC Black 310 (2)
Use one strand throughout

This blue sampler is built up from repeat patterns, many of which were used in household furnishings.

Design size: 28.5 x 47.5cm (11¼ x 18¾in)

Fabric: Aida 16 count, antique white

Thread: DMC Blue 336 (3)

Use one strand throughout

Chart for the top of the embroidery – this way up

Chart for the middle of the embroidery – this way up

Chart for the bottom of the embroidery – this way up

The main theme of this sampler is flowers, especially honeysuckle and roses.

Design size: 28.5 x 47.5cm (11¼ x 18¾in)

Fabric: Aida 16 count, antique white

Thread: DMC Dark Red 815 (3)

Use one strand throughout

Chart for the top of the embroidery – this way up

Chart for the middle of the embroidery – this way up

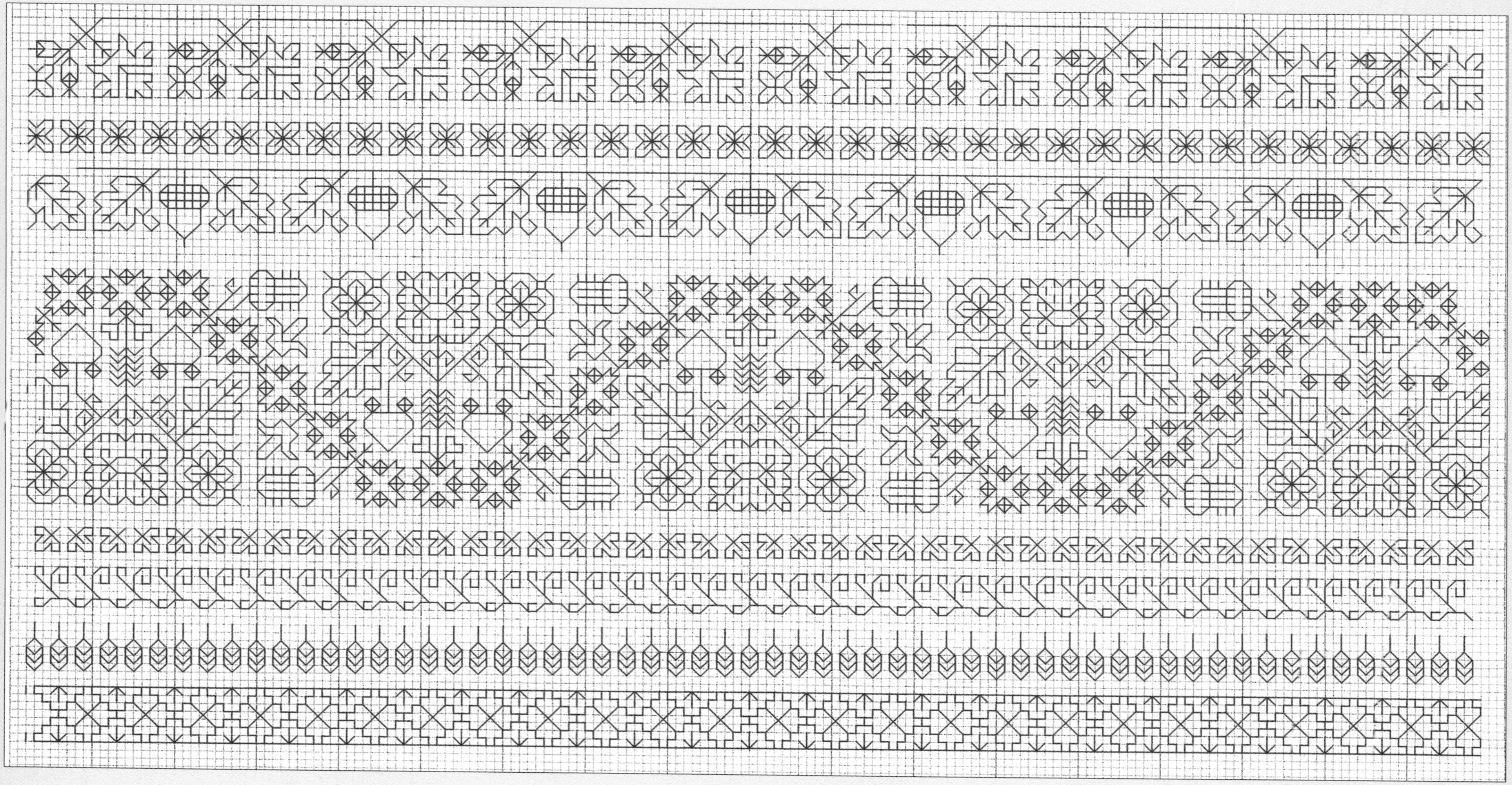

Chart for the bottom of the embroidery – this way up

Figures, birds and animals

By the end of the sixteenth century, books were becoming available, and they served as pattern sources for the embroiderer. This source became an important factor for the character and development of Elizabethan embroidery. The books covered subjects such as natural history, botanical and herbal, and the exotic plants, animals and birds that were being encountered by explorers of the New World. Creatures such as monkeys, camels, parrots, elephants and crocodiles began to appear in embroideries, as well as mythical creatures like the phoenix and the unicorn. Other sources such as wallpaper books and woodcut patterns for printing were also used for ideas by the embroiderer. Designs were transferred from the book to the fabric by punching tiny holes in the printed page, following the outline of the shape. The page was then placed on to the fabric and dusted with charcoal to produce a dotted outline. This technique was known as pouncing, and is one reason why so few of these early source books for embroidery designs have survived.

Figures were not used as much as birds and animals. Most of them, it is believed, had a symbolic meaning, such as the boxer or, as it was sometimes called, the lover or Renaissance Cupid. This figure often appears to be holding something such as a flower in its hand, as though bearing a gift. It may also have represented Adam.

This embroidery was inspired by band patterns characteristic of the sixteenth and seventeenth centuries. The top bands show stags and figures holding flowers. These were sometimes known as boxers because of their stance, or as lovers bearing gifts.

Mythical and exotic beasts featured alongside more commonplace animals in blackwork design.

This sampler includes many commonplace English motifs such as goats, ducks and acorns, as well as a human figure who may have represented Adam.

Design size: 11.5 x 24cm (4½ x 9½in)
Fabric: Aida 16 count, antique white
Threads: DMC Green 501
Orange 3776
Yellow 742
Pink 3726
Brown 839
Blue 931
Use one strand throughout

Figures like the ones shown were worked in back stitch or running stitch. They were often shown carrying acorns, flowers or heart-shaped objects, which may have suggested that they were bearing gifts. These figures have also been referred to as Cupids.

Design size: 10.7 x 7.7cm (4¼ x 3in)

Fabric: Aida 16 count, antique white

Thread: DMC Black 315 (1)
Gold 5282 (1)

Some people believe that pairs of figures like these represented Adam and Eve. These two are certainly in a beautiful garden!

Design size: 11.5 x 6.5cm (4½ x 2⅝in)

Fabric: Aida 16 count, antique white

Thread: DMC Grey 414 (1)
Pink 3350 (1)
Green 986 (1)
Dark Brown 839 (1)
Light Brown 783 (1)
Orange 3776 (1)
Gold 5282 (1)

This sampler is based on motifs from woodcut illustrations.

Design size: 18.5 x 20.5cm (7¼ x 8⅛in)

Fabric: Aida 16 count, chino

Thread: DMC Brown 839 (1)

Gold 5282 (1)

A variety of insects and small animals which would have been traced from available books, or inspired directly by the contents of the garden.

Design size: 16.5 x 24cm (6½ x 9½in)
Fabric: Aida 16 count, antique white
Threads: DMC Black 310 (1)

The outlines of the designs were sewn using back stitch.

Design size: 16 x 24.5cm (6¼ x 9⅝in)
Fabric: Aida 16 count, antique white
Thread: DMC Black 310 (1)

Fill-in patterns

If you have a design in mind that you would like to fill with various blackwork patterns, choose your first project carefully and do not be too ambitious. The simplest of shapes can become very impressive when finished. The following fill-in patterns are all shown in squares, but you can progress to more decorative shapes like the oak leaf

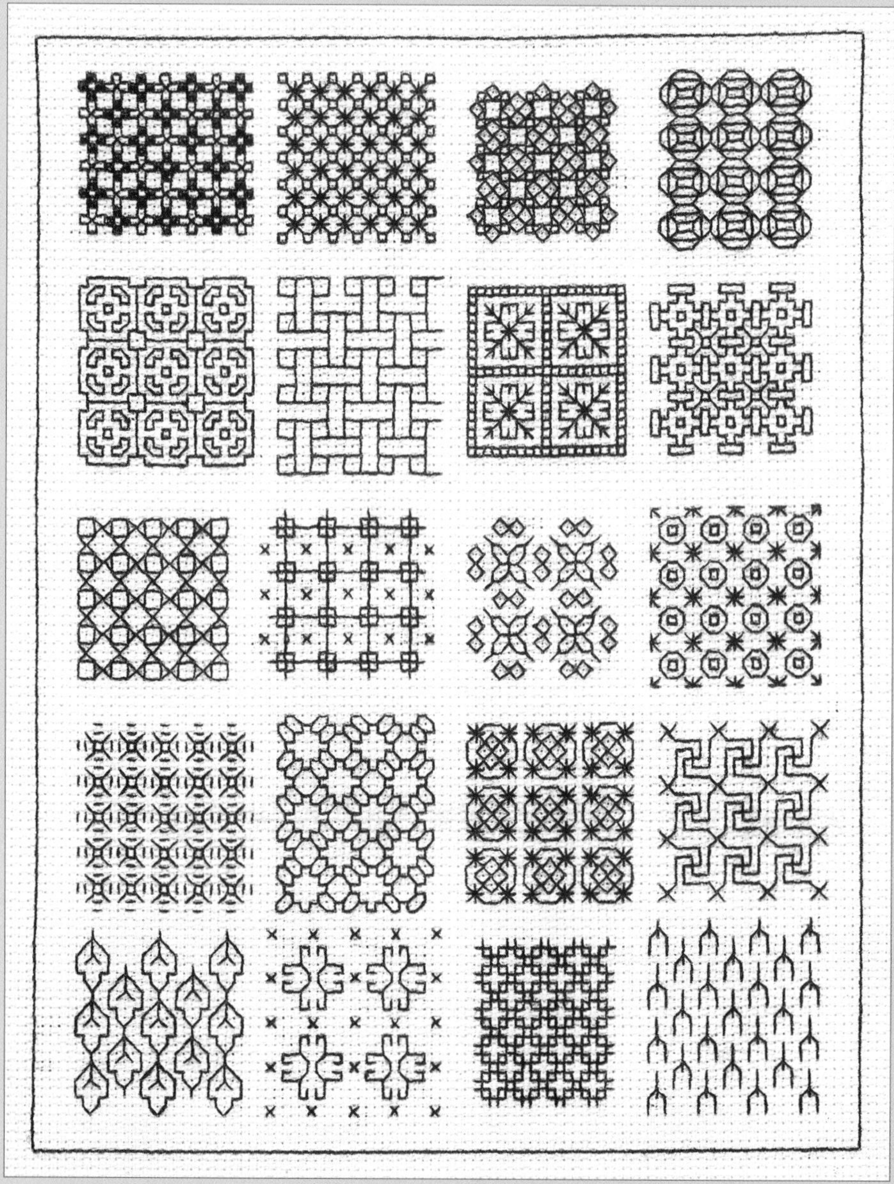

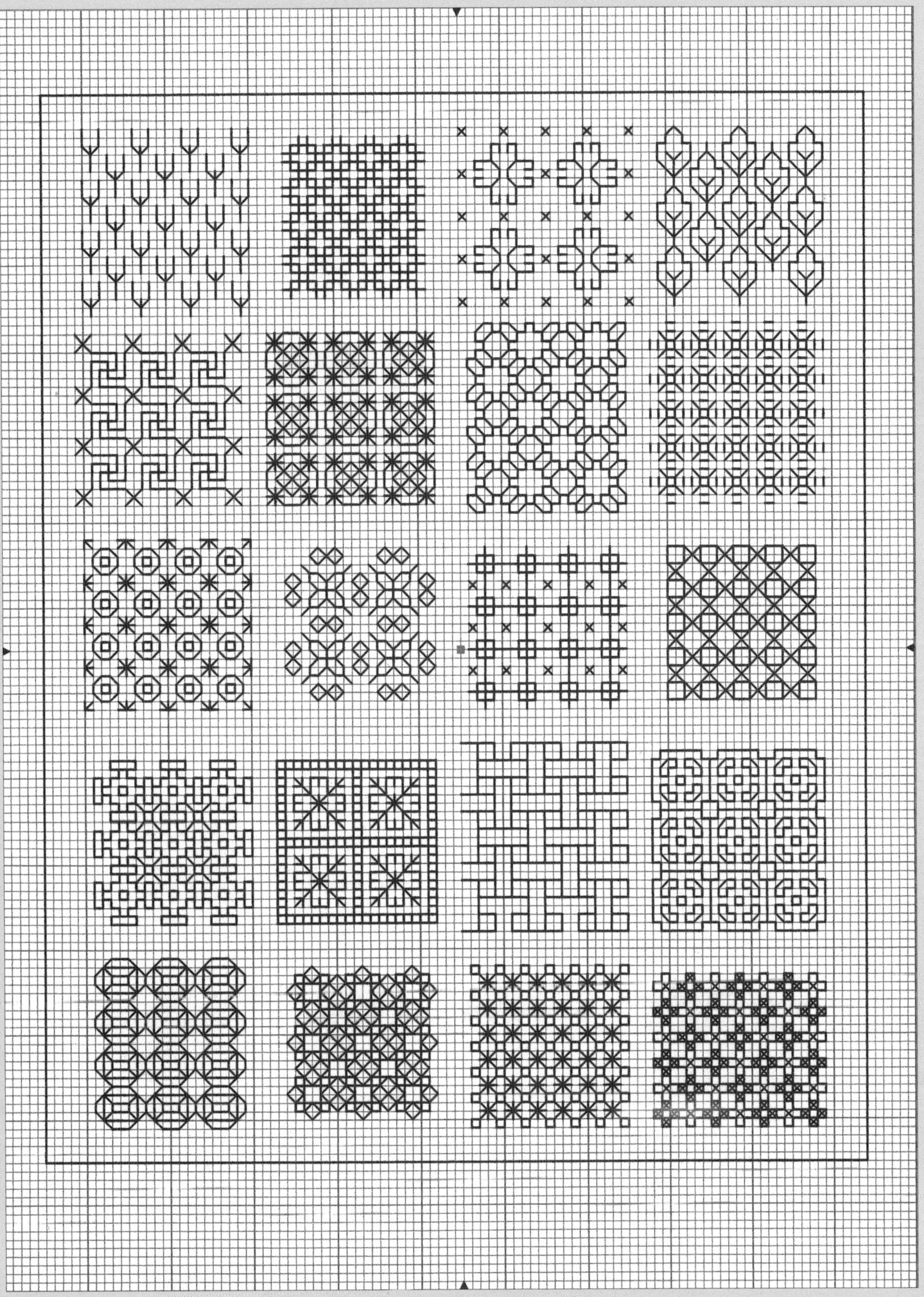

A design for a fill-in pattern may be created from one small motif, which is then multiplied, as in some of the patterns shown below.

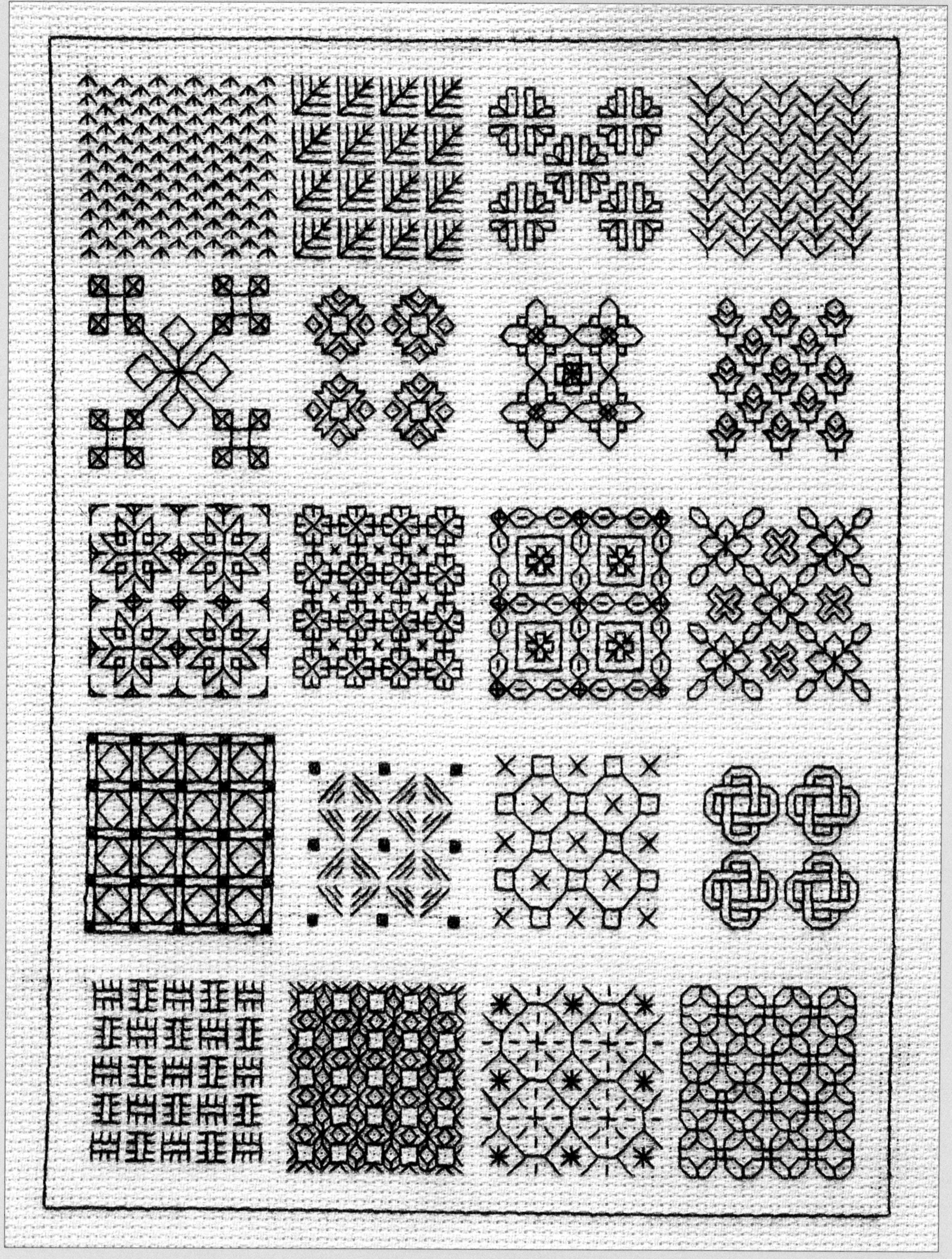

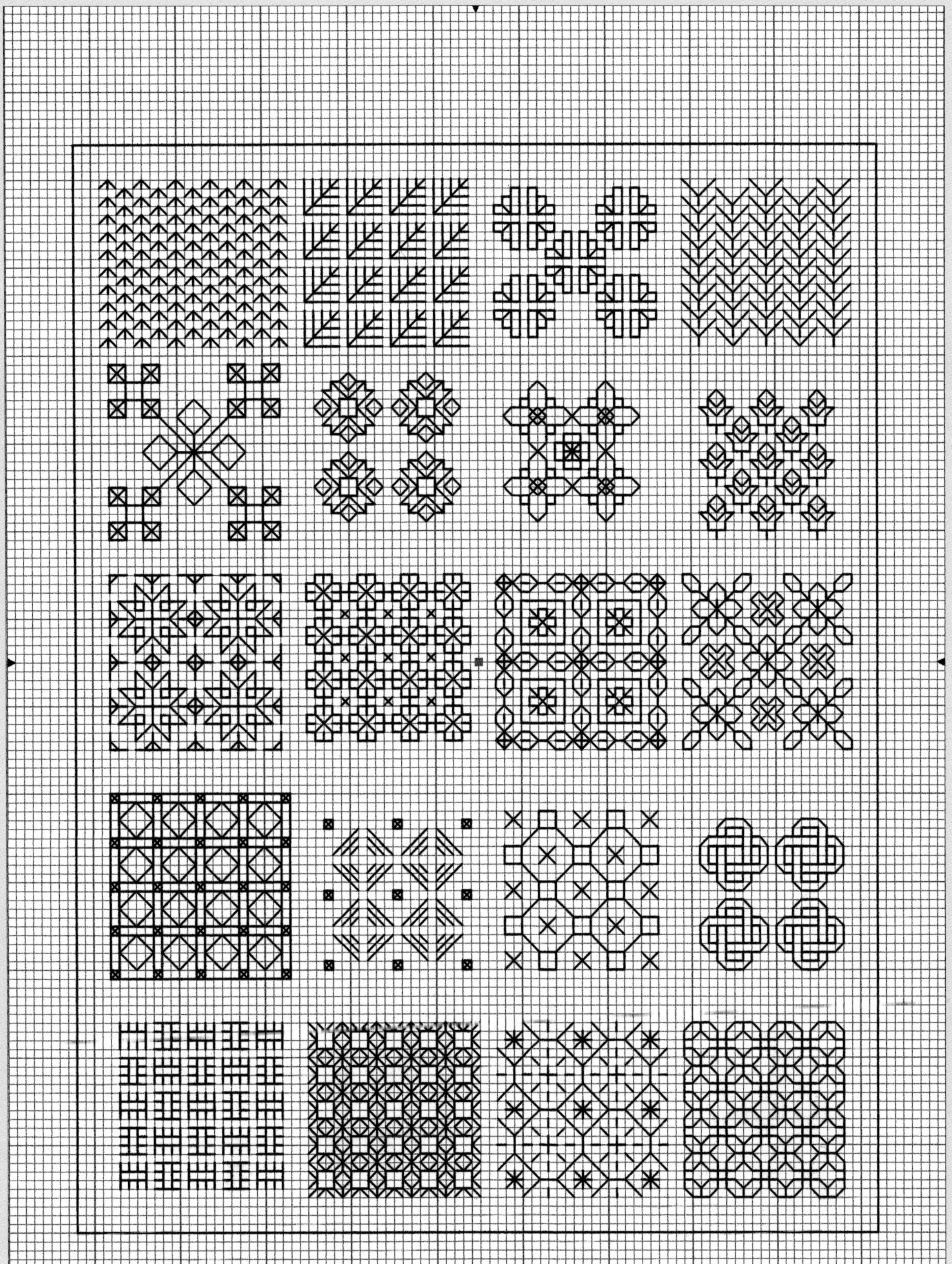

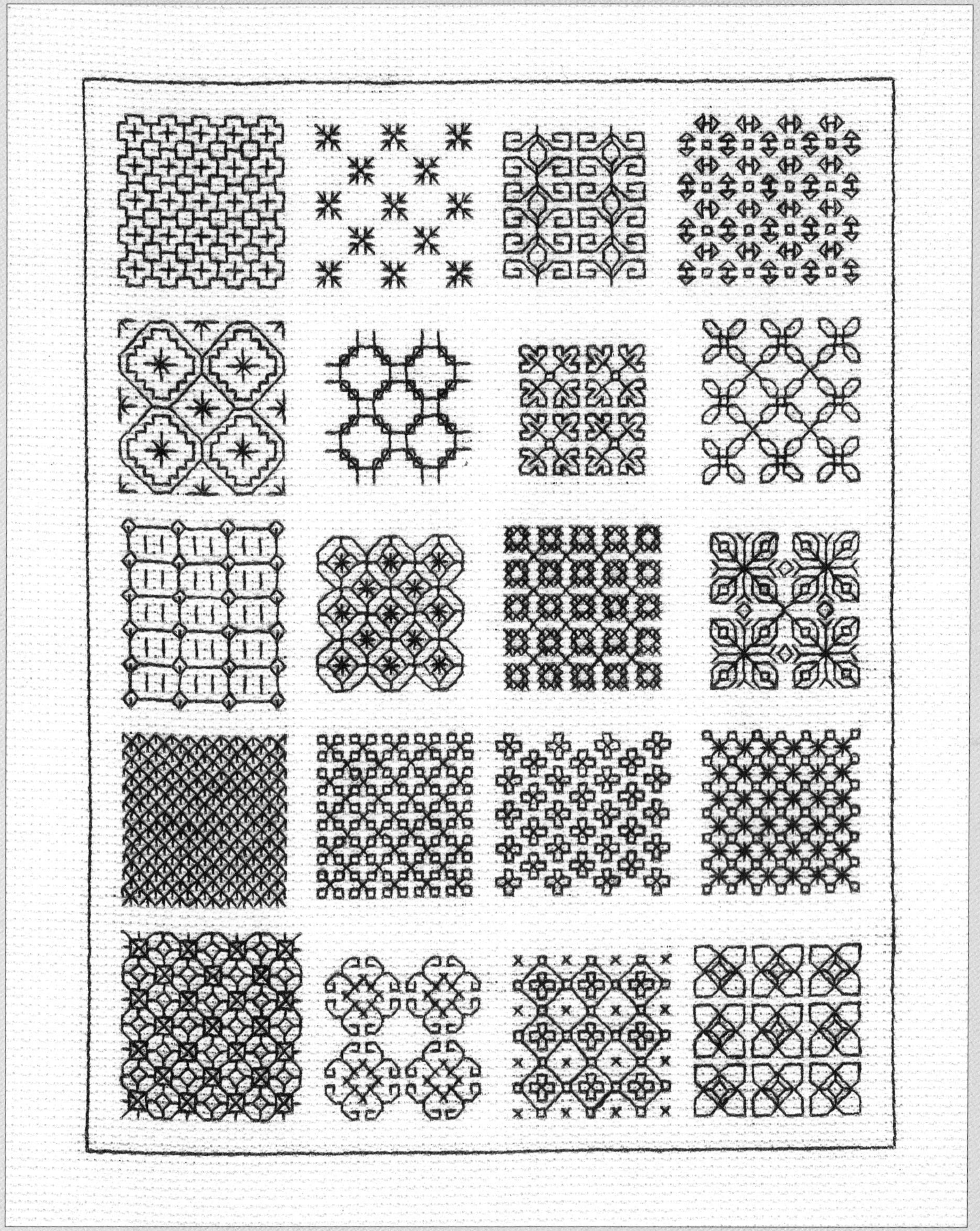

A close pattern will appear very dark, and an open pattern will look much lighter. When you need shadow in a design to create depth and form, the choice of pattern is therefore very important.

Inspiration for patterns can be found in objects such as iron gates or stained-glass windows.

This oak leaf shape is a good example of the use of fill-in patterns. I took this idea from one of the embroideries at Hardwick Hall, Derbyshire. As you can see, if you take one single leaf shape, then repeat and reverse the design and fill the same shape with different patterns, the end result is most effective.

Borders

In the fifteenth and sixteenth centuries, repeating patterns were used to decorate clothing. The smaller borders were used mainly for edging garments, creating a reinforced edge to the material. Larger borders were found on household linen and furnishings.

In the hundred years between Katharine of Aragon's arrival in England in 1501, and 1603 when Queen Elizabeth I died, blackwork underwent a remarkable transformation. At the beginning, there were only simple bands of decoration. Then, as time went on, with the development of printing, calligraphy and communications, the decoration of garments became more exuberant.

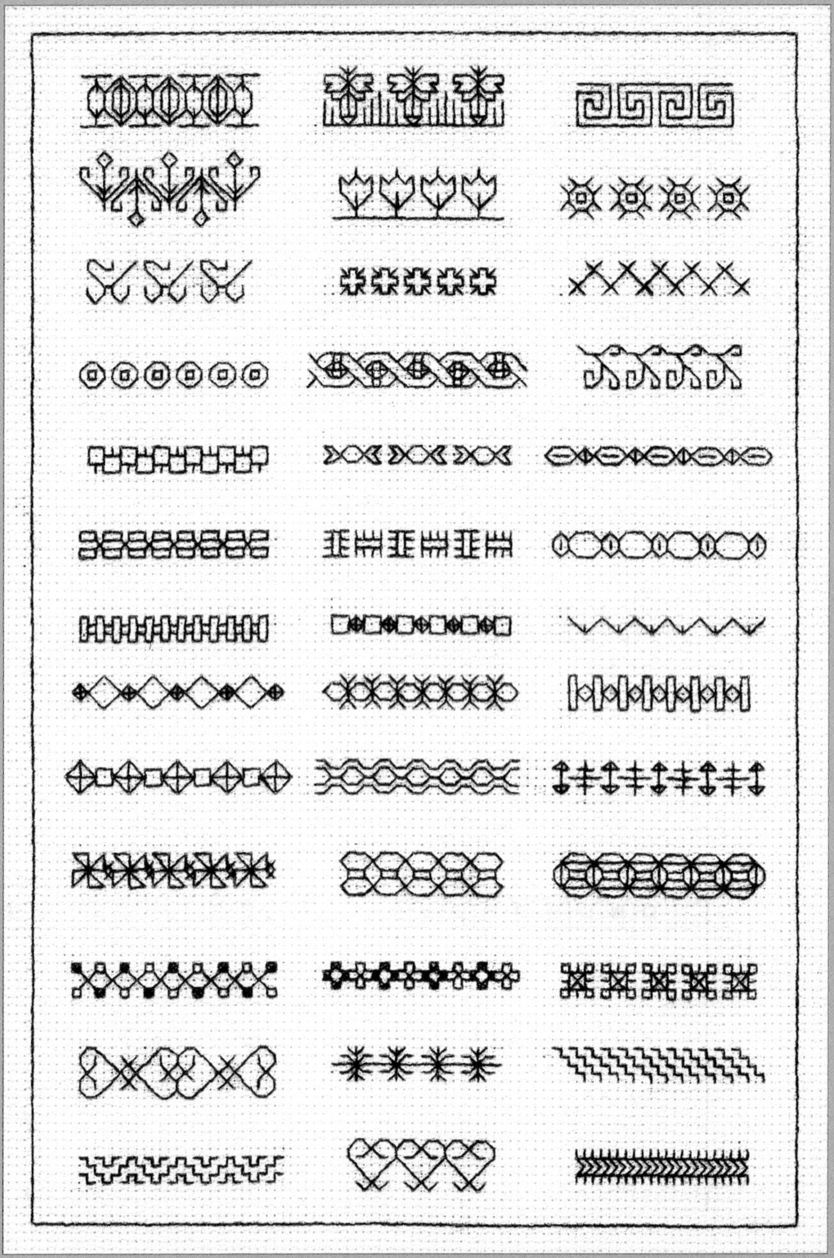

Smaller border designs like these were used to edge garments. Some of the patterns were so intricate that they resembled lace. Since lace was extremely expensive, blackwork was an ideal substitute. For the hard-working poor, it was a cheap way to reinforce the edges of cuffs and collars, while for the gentry it was a popular way to decorate caps, headdresses and gowns.

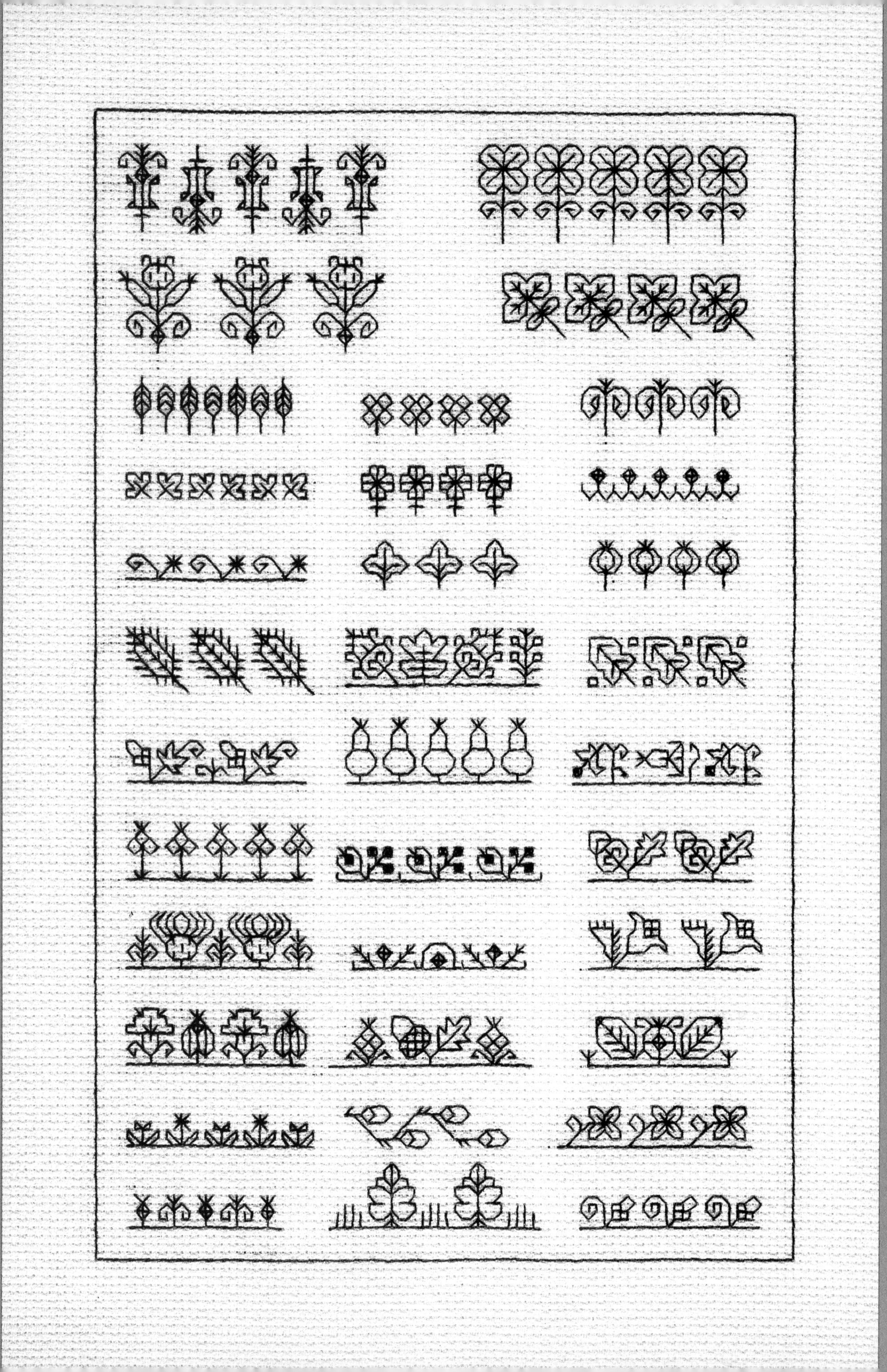

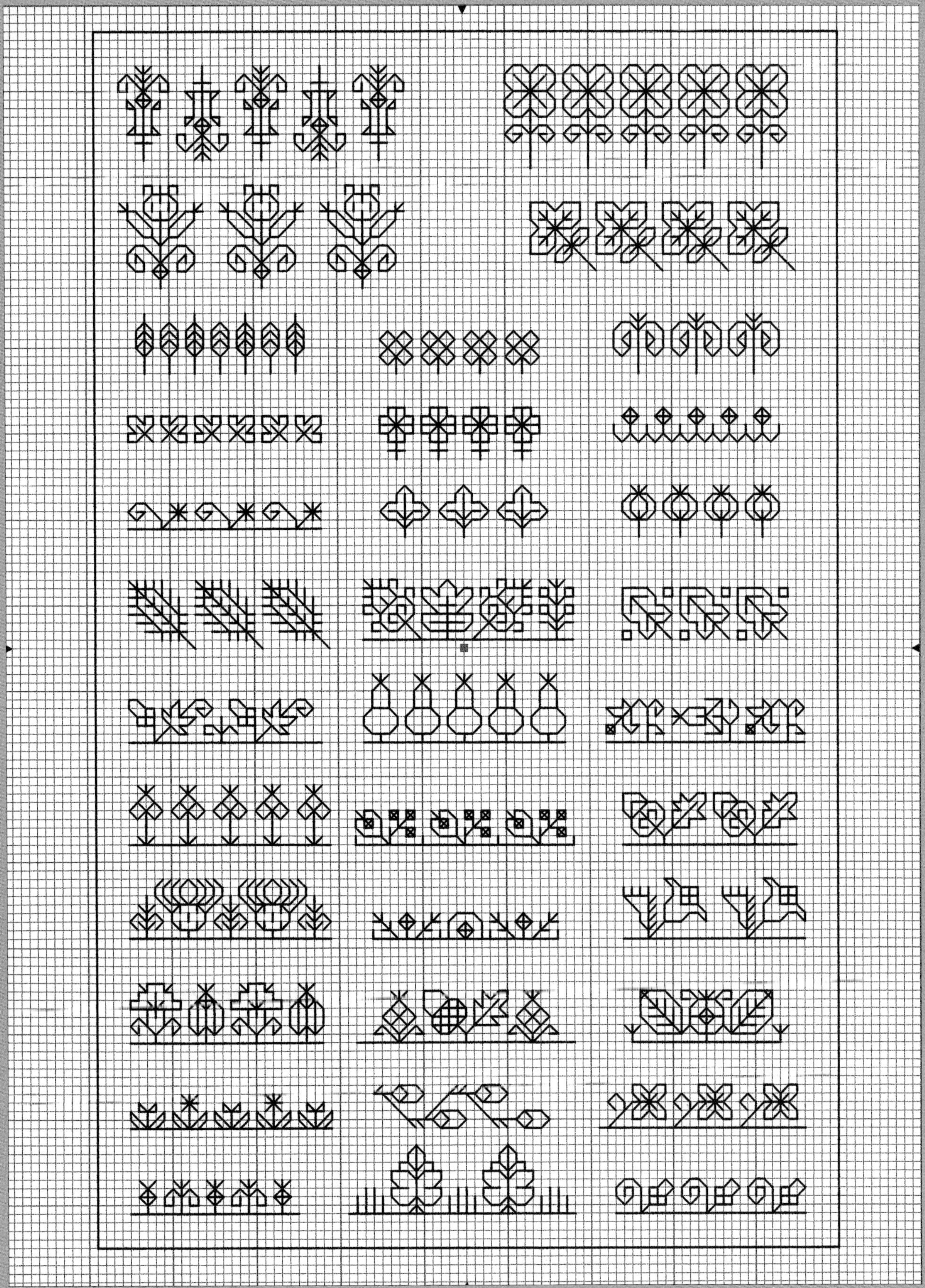

Larger borders like these were used on bed linen and other household items, and had practical as well as decorative uses. When the courts moved from place to place, a particular blackwork design would identify ownership, at a time when most people would have been unable to read written labels.

Most of the repeated motifs used in borders such as these had some kind of religious significance, were used as heraldic emblems, or derived from ancient legends or folklore. Others were simply taken from everyday items and had no particular meaning.

Here, bird, flower and plant motifs are repeated to create intricate borders.

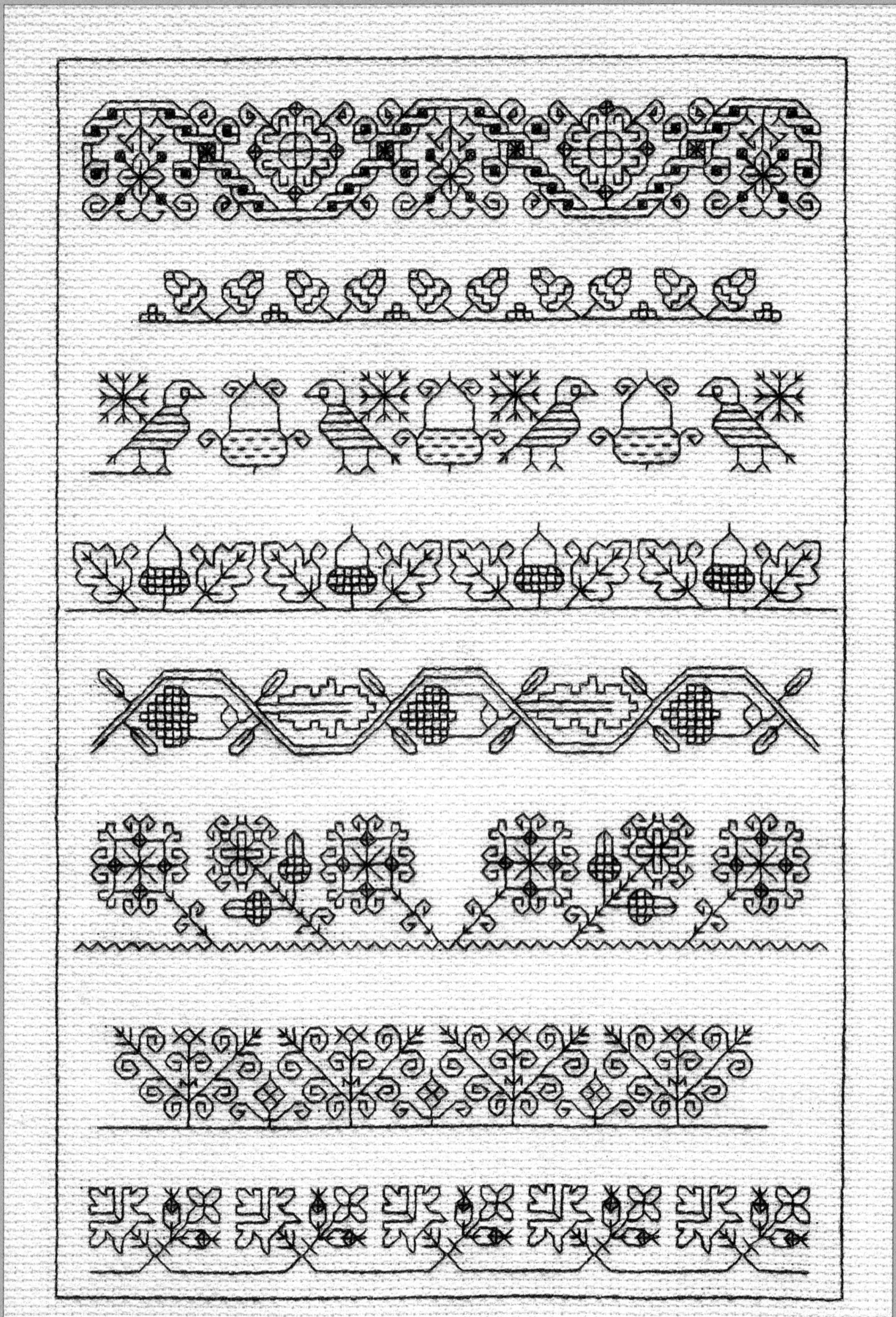

Flower and plant borders

Flowers and plants found in everyday surroundings were a popular theme in blackwork borders, which were used on household furnishings as well as clothing.

Border designs featuring flowers, thistles, acorns and knotwork shapes are combined in this band sampler.

Design size: 16.5 x 24.5cm (6½ x 9⅝in)

Fabric: Aida 16 count, antique white

Thread:

DMC Dark Pink 3350 (1)
Orange 3776 (1)
Light Green 470 (1)
Dark Green 986 (1)
Mauve 553 (1)
Brown 801 (1)

A variety of flowers including the iris, artichoke and pansy appear in this sampler.
Design size: 17 x 21cm (6¾ x 8¼in)
Fabric: Aida 16 count, antique white
Thread: DMC Light Pink 3733 (1)
Dark Pink 3350 (1)
Orange 3776 (1)
Light Green 470 (1)
Dark Green 986 (1)
Mauve 553 (1)
Blue 780 (1)

Smaller borders like these were originally used on the edges of clothing, such as on the cuffs, to provide extra reinforcement.

Design size: 16.5 x 24cm (6½ x 9½in)

Fabric: Aida 16 count, antique white

Thread: DMC Light Pink 3733 (1)

Dark Pink 3350 (1)

Orange 3776 (1)

Light Green 470 (1)

Dark Green 986 (1)

Mauve 553 (1)

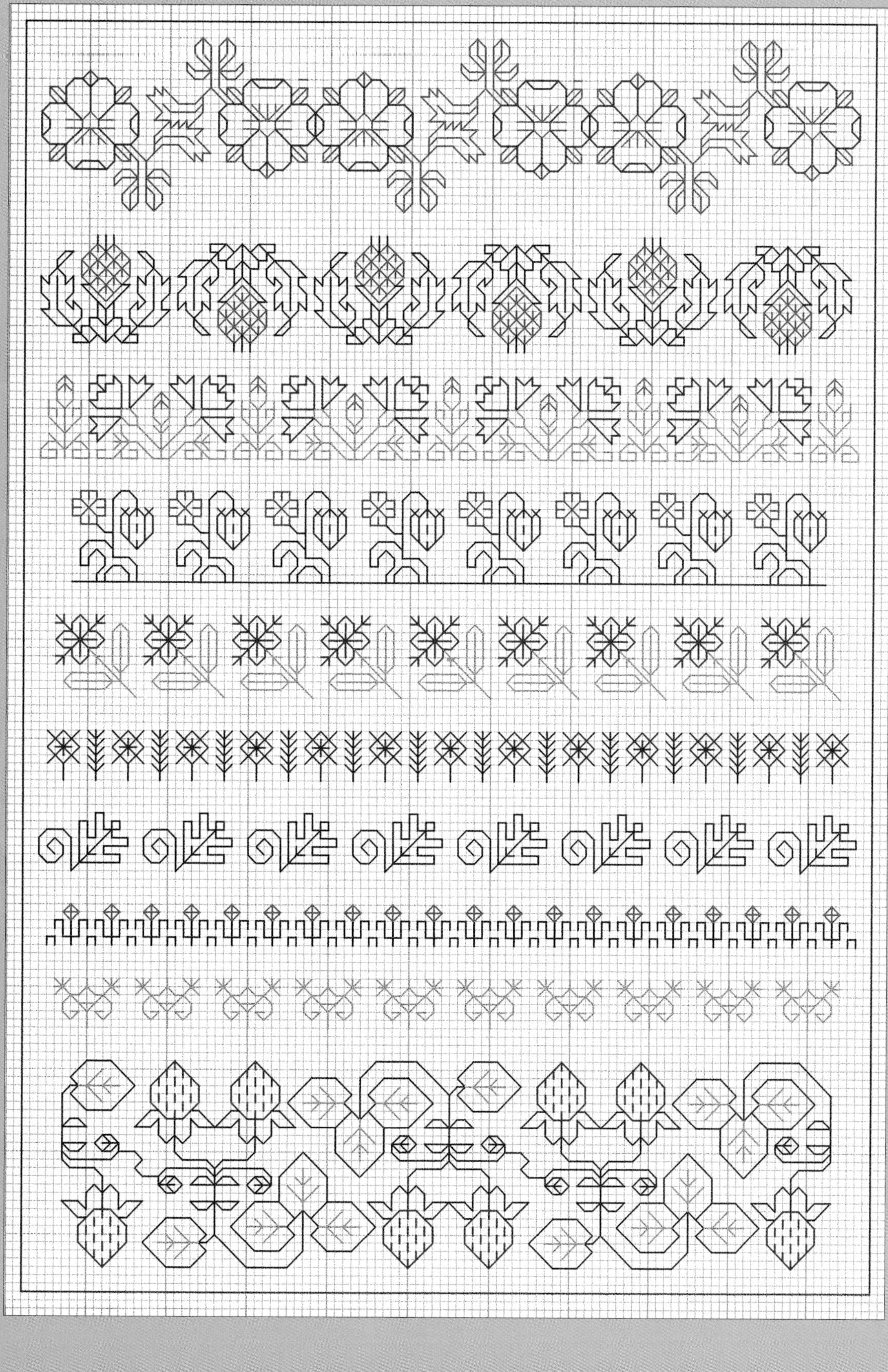

Alphabets

Alphabets were not a great feature of blackwork embroidery, except for the marking of household linen, but they became more popular towards the seventeenth century, when they were used for schoolroom purposes.

On many of the samplers the letters I, J, U, V and W were omitted. This may have been because the Latin alphabet left out J, V and W. V was the capital form of U and J was not used until the mid-nineteenth century. J evolved from the letter I, which had appeared in the fourteenth century and was still used only occasionally during the sixteenth.

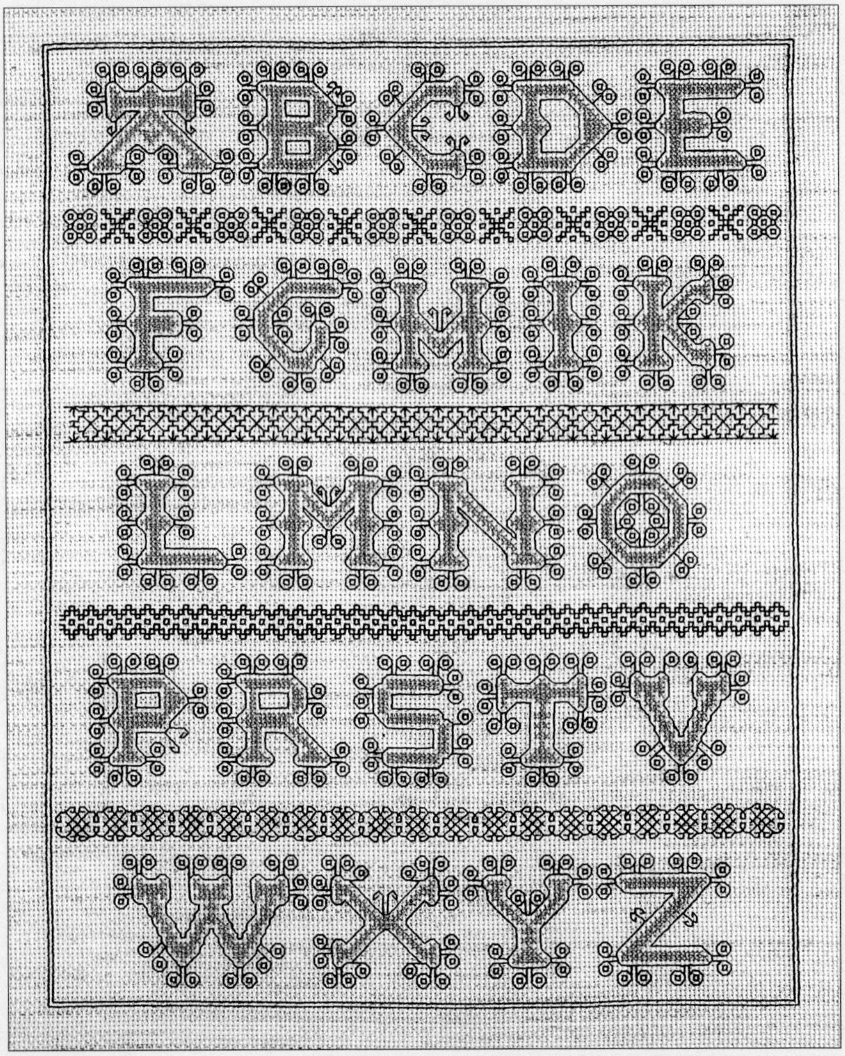

The letters from this sampler can also be used individually, to adorn a small object such as a pincushion.

Design size: 22 x 27.3cm ($8^5/_8$ x $10^3/_4$in)

Fabric: Aida 18 count, Chino

Thread: DMC Brown 801 (1) Gold 5282 (1)

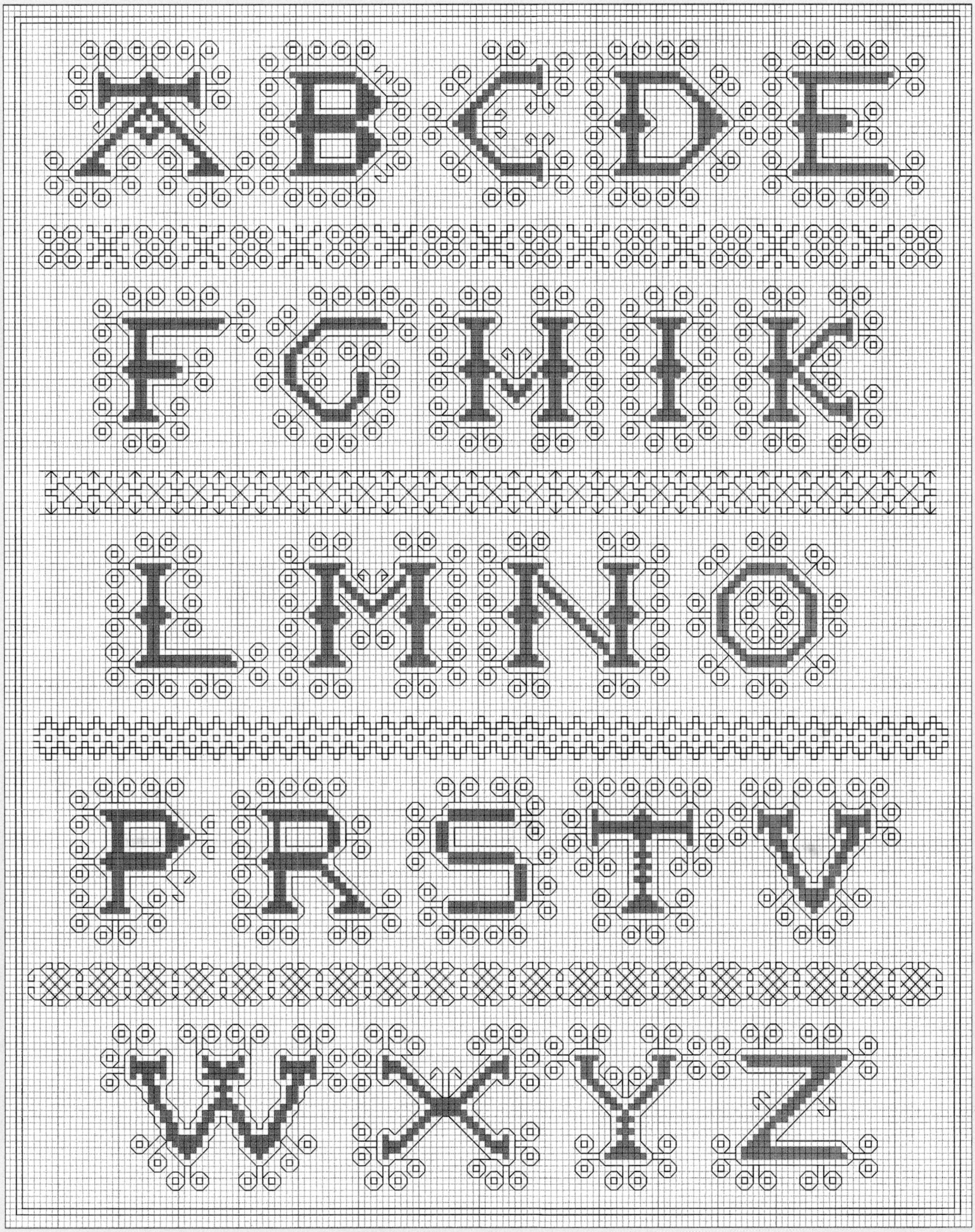

Less ornate letters and numbers like these were used mainly for the marking of household linen.
Design size: 13.5 x 19.7cm (5³/₈ x 7¾in)

Fabric: Aida 16 count, antique white
Thread: DMC Black 310 (1)
Pink 3350 (1)

ABCDEFGHIJKLMNOPQR
STUVWXYZ
abcdefghijklmnopqrstuvwxyz
1234567890
ABCDEFGHIJKLMNOPQRSTUVWXYZ
1234567890
ABCDEFGHIJKLM
NOPQRSTUVWXYZ
abcdefghijklmnopqrstuvwxyz
1234567890
ABCDEFGHIJKLMN
OPQRSTUVWXYZ
1234567890

Alphabets like this one are not particularly common in blackwork, but they do occasionally appear on household items, where, like borders, they may have been used to identify the owner.

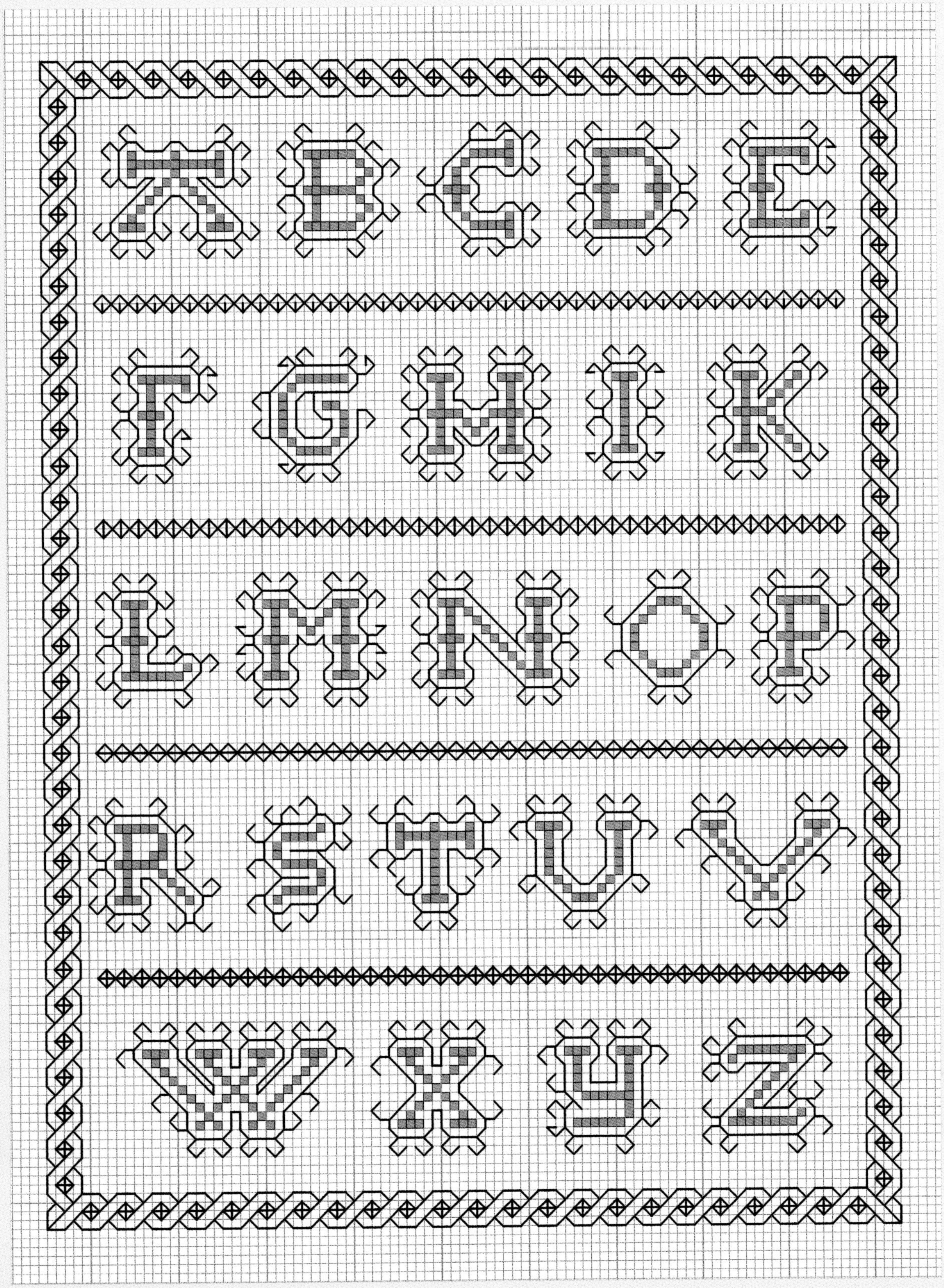
A B C D E
F G H I K
L M N O P
R S T U V
W X Y Z

Mounting your work

When you have completed your embroidery, if you have decided to frame and display it, you will need to follow these basic guidelines. Use a white acid-free mounting board, available from good stationery or art shops. You will need to know the exact size of the picture frame before cutting the board, so it will fit nicely inside the frame.

1. Place the embroidery face-down and cover it with a fine, dry cloth. Apply a warm iron gently and lightly so that the stitches are not flattened or distorted.

2. When you have decided how much of your embroidery you wish to frame, cut your mounting board to this measurement, using a craft knife and a cutting board.

3. Measure the mounting board horizontally and vertically to find the centre. Push a needle through this centre point so that the point just comes through to the other side.

4. Measure the embroidery in the same way to find the centre point of the design, and push the eye of the needle on the mounting board through this point, so that the centre of the design is positioned accurately on the centre of the board.

5. When you are happy that the board is central, place pins through the fabric at the board's edges, sticking outwards so that the board can be turned over easily.

6. Trim the excess fabric to about 5cm (2in) all round and turn the embroidery over, face down.

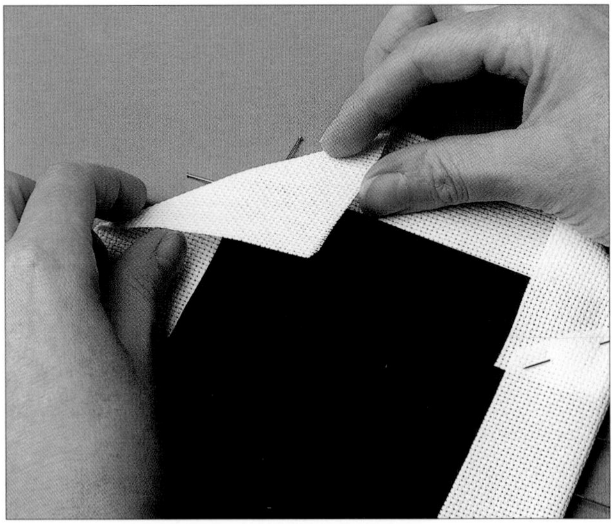

7. Mitre the corners, fold in the sides and pin them down.

8. Sew the edges of the fabric together at each corner. Remove the pins.

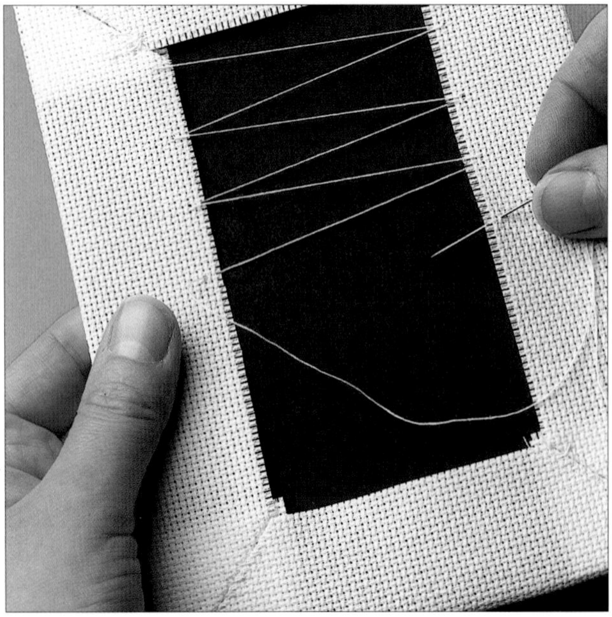

9. Fix the edges of the fabric in place with double-sided tape, or lace across the back using a strong thread.

10. Remove the pins and place the mount in the picture frame.

The mounted, framed embroidery.

Another framed piece.

Index